SIMPLIFY YOUR
Wedding

A **Reader's Digest Simpler Life**™ Book

Designed, edited, and produced by Weldon Owen

THE READER'S DIGEST ASSOCIATION, INC.

Executive Editor, Trade Books Joseph Gonzalez
Senior Design Director, Trade Books Henrietta Stern
Project Editor Candace Conard
Project Art Director Jane Wilson

WELDON OWEN INC.

President John Owen
Publisher Roger S. Shaw
Series Editor Janet Goldenberg
Managing Editor Dianne Jacob
Contributing Editors Bonnie Monte, Vicki Webster
Copy Editors Lisa R. Bornstein, Gail Nelson

Art Director Emma Forge
Senior Designer Elizabeth Marken
Production Designer Brynn Breuner
Design Assistant William Erik Evans
Icon Illustrator Matt Graif

Production Director Stephanie Sherman
Production Manager Jen Dalton

Project Photographers Chris Shorten, Brian Pierce
Photo Stylist JoAnn Masaoka Van Atta
Photo Editor Anne Stovell

A Reader's Digest/Weldon Owen Publication
Copyright © 1998 The Reader's Digest Association, Inc., and Weldon Owen Inc.

Library of Congress Cataloging in Publication Data
Baroni, Allana.
    Simplify your wedding / Allana Baroni.
        p.   cm. — (Simpler life)
    Includes index.
    ISBN 0-7621-0063-x
    1. Weddings—Planning.   2. Wedding etiquette.   I. Title.
II. Series.
HQ745.B375   1998
395.2'2—dc21   98-11144

Printed in China

A note on weights and measures: Metric equivalences given for
U.S. weights and measures are approximate. Actual equivalences may vary.

SIMPLIFY YOUR
Wedding

ALLANA BARONI

Illustrations by TOM PAYNE

Reader's Digest

The Reader's Digest Association, Inc.
Pleasantville, New York/Montreal

CONTENTS

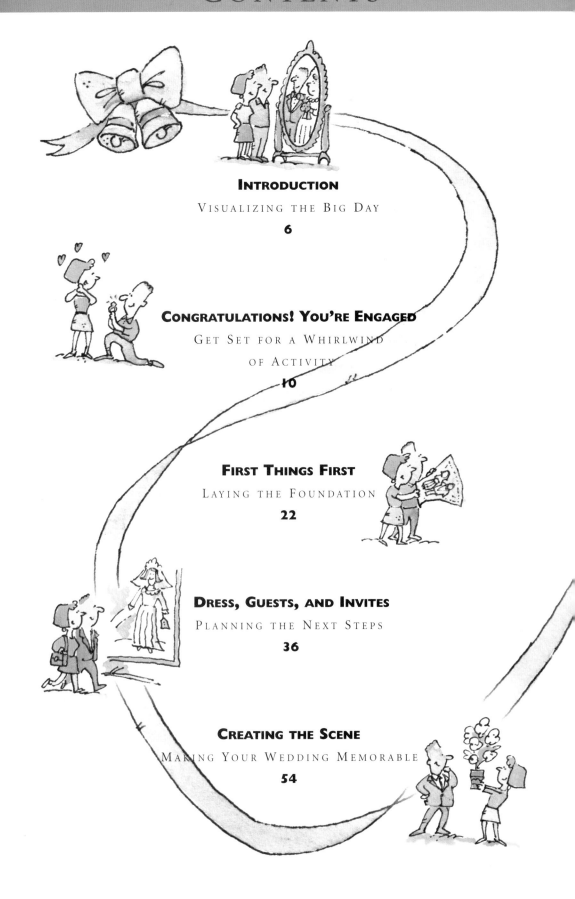

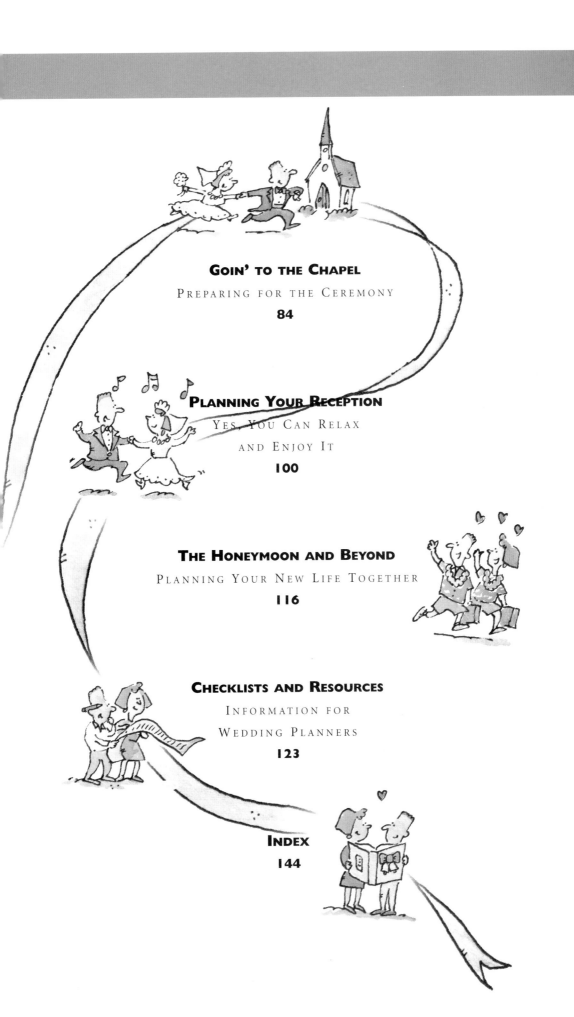

Planning is easier if you visualize
your wedding event by event.

Visualizing
the Big Day

——————*

What is it about planning a wedding that evokes such a flurry of excitement, anticipation—and anxiety? Is it because marriage is a new beginning that every detail seems to take on special significance? One thing is certain: As a symbol of the perfect union, a wedding speaks to the optimist in us all. We enter into a marriage full of love for another person. Maybe that's why every couple wants their event to be perfect.

This handbook can help you have the wedding of your dreams without losing your sanity in the process. During my career as an entertaining and bridal consultant, I've favored an uncomplicated approach to planning, even for the most lavish affair. Simplicity, after all, doesn't mean skimping on flair. It means stripping away the steps that only add work and time. I'll show you how to pare down the planning to what is essential and how to skip the unnecessary extras.

Much of the fun comes from knowing you are creating an event unlike any other. Making the occasion truly your own is as simple as including the things that are important to you—hosting your wedding at a location with personal significance, reading a special poem during your ceremony, including friends and relatives in the ceremony in surprising ways, or adding family recipes to your reception menu. The many simple ways to personalize your celebration will become evident as you read, and with each suggestion you'll find easy, manageable steps for achieving maximum results with minimum effort. From announcing your engagement, to choosing invitations, music, food, clothing, and decor, these pages offer a wealth of ideas to make your wedding truly unique.

Simplify Your Wedding is packed with easy-to-follow techniques and plans that I've gleaned during my career—hints that will save you time, money, and stress. Negotiating with vendors is new territory for many couples, but I'll guide you through the entire process. You'll find lists of questions to ask caterers, florists, photographers, and other vendors; photos to inspire you with ideas for the decor; and suggestions for romantic honeymoons. You'll even find advice on giving toasts. And the checklists at the back ensure that you won't forget a thing along the way. Your wedding—from planning to the final toast—*can* be simple and stress-free.

Weddings are joyous occasions, especially for the bride and groom. So relax, and have the time of your lives.

Remember that all the effort of planning pays off
when you start your new life with the person you love!

SIMPLE SYMBOLS

---- ✳ ----

BECAUSE YOU'RE BUSY, you're unlikely to have enough time to read this book from cover to cover. That's why it's packed with concise capsules of information, perfect for digesting in small pieces. In these tip boxes you'll find practical ideas to help you accomplish your tasks more quickly, more simply, or less expensively. Each tip category is marked with its own symbol. Here's what the symbols mean:

 Labor Savers provide advice on how to delegate jobs, share the responsibilities, or skip non-essentials altogether. There are a million and one details that go into planning a wedding, so it's worthwhile saving your energy for what really matters.

 Stress Busters provide simple, surefire methods to eliminate worry every step of the way. There's really no need for frazzled nerves or sleepless nights if you keep an eye out for these easy strategies that will keep things humming along.

 Time Savers present quick solutions to save you that most precious of commodities: your time. Refer to these shortcuts to slice minutes—even hours—from your work time without compromising the style, mood, or excitement of your day.

 Cost Cutters offer practical ways to save money without sacrificing style. Whether the wedding is simple or opulent, every couple can use some help staying within the budget. Use the savings you find in one area to splurge in another.

 Bright Ideas are the sort of secrets that professional bridal consultants rely on to make the whole planning process go smoothly. Get smart with these insider tips: places to register for gifts, choosing the perfect wedding date, and more.

 Rules of Thumb are time-honored principles that help you eliminate the guesswork when calculating budgets and quantities. These are the sort of tricks that professionals use when orchestrating any event, regardless of its size.

 Simply Safer tips make safety rules easy to follow. Although weddings might seem low on the danger scale, there are always some hazards wherever crowds congregate. Keep these simple precautions in mind as you arrange the many details of your ceremony, reception, and honeymoon.

 Don't Forget tips offer items to remember that may seem obvious at first but that are all too easy to forget amid the hustle and bustle of planning a wedding. Refer to these suggestions to ensure that everything goes according to plan and that nothing essential gets left out along the way.

SHARE the
Excitement

—✳—

1 Announce your **engagement** to family and close friends first. Make it special—send a telegram, or write the message in icing on a cake. **2** If you're selecting **wedding bands** for each other, you could have them engraved with your initials and the wedding date, or add a short, special message. **3** When choosing the **wedding party,** resist outside pressure and select only people you feel comfortable with. **4** Consider hiring a wedding **consultant** to take some of the pressure off. **5** Make it easier for your guests by **registering** for wedding gifts. Set up an appointment with the store consultant, who will browse through the store with you, offering advice and guidance. **6** Invite your wedding party over for an informal working lunch to discuss **planning** for the big day. Serve something simple and start assigning tasks. **7** Pace prewedding parties so you both have a chance to catch your breath in between. The point of such parties is to **have fun,** not to be worn out before the event. ●

CONGRATULATIONS!
YOU'RE ENGAGED

GET SET FOR A WHIRLWIND OF ACTIVITY

* —— * —— *

Now that you and your spouse-to-be have made the big decision, the fun part is about to begin: spreading the news, arranging the wedding, and attending a round of parties to celebrate this important occasion. Even if you've planned only a brief engagement, don't worry; everything will get done. Try to take it easy and move ahead one step at a time.

One pleasure of preparing for your wedding is choosing the wedding party. Originally, the role of the attendants was to escort the bride and groom safely to the location of the ceremony. Today it's a way to have your closest friends and relatives participate in your excitement.

Registering for gifts is another high point of the preparations. It provides a rare opportunity to pick out the things you'd like most for your new home. Be creative with your registry, and choose only the items that you really want.

Now relax, and enjoy being the center of all the attention.

TELLING FAMILY AND FRIENDS

───── ✳ ─────

E VEN IF YOU HAVEN'T SET A WEDDING DATE YET, DON'T LET THAT STOP YOU FROM ANNOUNCING YOUR ENGAGEMENT TO RELATIVES AND FRIENDS. ONCE YOU'VE CHOSEN A DATE, ASSEMBLE THE "TEAM." LATER ON, REGISTER FOR GIFTS.

Many couples announce their engagement at a formal dinner, but there are plenty of simpler ways to convey the news. You can send telegrams, surprise your family with an impromptu visit (either alone or with your fiancé), or write the message in icing on a cake. You may want to tell your parents in person.

There's no set rule for filling in your friends. Depending on your preferences and how far away friends live, you might tell them in person, make a flurry of excited phone calls, dash off faxes or e-mail, write letters or postcards, or mail formal written announcements.

Running a newspaper announcement is easy. Most papers have forms that specify what information they want. Simply contact the newspaper's lifestyle or society desk to inquire about specifics, deadlines, and photograph requirements.

Some couples host their own engagement parties without telling guests the reason, then announce their big news at the gathering.

Once word gets out, you might be treated to an engagement party or two. Traditionally, the bride's parents were the hosts, but today it might be the groom's parents or other family members, close friends, even the best man. The party can be a picnic,

Surprise your family with an impromptu visit to break the news.

a barbecue, a cocktail party, a weekend brunch, a clambake, or dinner and a movie with a group. Some couples decide to host their own engagement party; they invite guests without giving the reason, then announce their big news at the gathering.

Gifts aren't mandatory at an engagement party, but if you do receive any, send a thank-you note promptly. Also thank the host for honoring you with a party.

CHOOSING RINGS

If the groom-to-be didn't pop the question with an engagement ring in hand, you'll want to go together to choose one (see the box at right). Although a classic-cut, sparkling diamond may be hard to resist, other stones, such as rubies, sapphires, emeralds, and pearls, capture the hearts of brides all over the world. An engagement ring can also include the bride's birthstone or a stone to commemorate the month in which you plan to marry.

The wedding band is perhaps the most recognized icon of marriage, symbolizing never-ending devotion. Typically, an engagement ring is more expensive than a wedding band. This is especially true if the engagement ring has a large diamond, several gemstones, or intricate detailing. Wedding bands usually have a simple design and are made of gold (this can be yellow, rose, or white), platinum, or silver. Platinum is the strongest of the three metals and the most expensive.

Shop for your rings at a reputable jeweler's. To set your mind at ease, request a certificate of authenticity and a written appraisal for the rings you choose. If you

RINGS THAT ARE IN FASHION ONE YEAR MAY LOOK OUTDATED THE NEXT. TAKE THE UNCERTAINTY OUT OF THE SELECTION PROCESS BY CHOOSING CLASSICS.

Engagement rings

An engagement ring is an investment you'll want to make with care. When selecting your diamond, consider the "four Cs": carat, cut, clarity, and color. *Carat* is a measurement of the stone's weight (1 carat equals $1/5$ of a gram). *Cut* refers to the way the stone is shaped and the number of facets it has. The round brilliant cut is the classic shape. Others are the pear shape, the marquise (elliptical, with pointed ends), and the rectangular or square emerald cut. *Clarity* measures a stone's freedom from imperfections—cracks, blemishes, debris, and bubbles. The highest rating is FL (flawless); the lowest, I (imperfect). *Color* ratings run from D (clear and colorless, usually the most expensive) to Z (with yellow or brown tones). Beyond Z there are "fancy-color" grades, including rare, valuable hues such as red and purple.

Wedding bands

There are no fixed rules for choosing the style and material, but a classic, unadorned band never goes out of fashion. Choose rings that are comfortable to wear daily. Personalize your bands by having them engraved with both of your initials and your wedding date.

want to purchase an antique, concentrate your search among estate jewelers and antique shops for a selection of rings with excellent craftsmanship and design. If you have a specific idea in mind and can't find it, design your own rings and have them made by a reputable craftsperson.

ASSEMBLING THE TEAM

You can plan your wedding and have a blast doing it. But forget the "I can do it all" philosophy. This is no time to be a superhero. Delegate chores to the wedding party, friends, and professionals.

The wedding party is the nucleus of your team. Traditionally it is made up of the bride, the groom, their attendants, the bride's honor attendant, the groom's best man, the flower girl, the ring bearer, pages or train bearers, and the parents of

Friends will be excited *at the news of your engagement and will want to help. Choose attendants you can really count on.*

the bride and groom. The bride's attendants are bridesmaids or bridal attendants; the groom's attendants are groomsmen or ushers—either term is correct. You can expand the wedding party to include anyone else you want, such as candle lighters and additional ushers.

If you would like your guests to be escorted to their seats and the groomsmen need help with the job, then enlist the help of other family and friends to act as ushers with the groomsmen. They don't have to be part of the procession that walks down the aisle.

> **Forget the "I can do it all" philosophy. Delegate chores to the wedding party, friends, and professionals.**

When you're selecting members of the wedding party, stick with close relatives and friends. Don't give in to pressure to include someone you're not comfortable working with. This is your wedding, and you should enjoy every moment.

To avoid hurting the feelings of any people you would rather not have in your wedding party, ask them to be "honorary participants." Invite them to all of the prewedding functions, assign them one or two duties each, and seat them in a special place of honor in the audience.

Don't worry about having an equal ratio of attendants to groomsmen; you can work out the procession and recession to accommodate uneven numbers. It's more important to consider your budget, since you'll need bouquets, boutonnieres, and gifts for all those involved (see page 32). Generally, the more formal the event, the larger the bridal party, so plan your cast of characters accordingly. Once you have chosen your wedding party, assign specific duties to each person.

INVOLVING ATTENDANTS

Confused about job definitions and what to assign to each person? Here's a breakdown of traditional roles and duties.

The honor attendant plays the role of confidante and offers moral support to the bride. This person holds the groom's ring during the ceremony, signs the marriage certificate as a witness, and helps the bride with her attire during and after the ceremony. This attendant is also known as matron of honor if married, maid of honor if unmarried, maiden of honor if a young girl, or (rarely) person of honor if male.

The simplest way to determine duties is to consider the honor attendant your second pair of hands. Often honor attendants help address invitations, assemble wedding favors, and arrange travel. They also schedule fittings for the bridesmaids, assist the bride with dressing on the day of the wedding, and take the bridal gown to the cleaners or to the bride's home afterward. Additionally, they might host the wedding shower and bachelorette party, along with the bridesmaids.

The best man lightens the groom's load of responsibilities and takes on the role of personal supporter. The job can be filled by anyone (male or female) who is close to the groom. Often best men arrange

The Art of Delegating Tasks

When you're assigning any responsibilities, consider each person's talents. If one of your friends has beautiful handwriting, invite her to address the envelopes. Ask your diplomatic sister-in-law-to-be for help with the seating chart. Keep a list of small tasks to assign honorary participants so they will feel that they are really part of the team, helping with many of the activities.

the bachelor party, see that the groomsmen are all properly fitted and dressed, make sure that the groom is properly dressed, get the groom to the ceremony on time, sign the certificate of marriage as a witness, carry the bride's ring during the ceremony, and act as the toastmaster at the reception. They might also arrange transportation, deliver the officiant's fee, return groom's and groomsmen's rented attire, or take the groom's attire to the cleaners.

Bridesmaids can offer to run errands and help with prewedding and wedding-day tasks. They may also cohost the bridal shower and bachelorette party.

Groomsmen offer assistance for any prewedding tasks. They may also cohost the bachelor party, act as ushers and seat guests before the ceremony, and unroll the aisle runner (if used).

Both bridesmaids and groomsmen attend the prewedding parties, act as troubleshooters for any problems that may arise on the wedding day, propose toasts to the bride and groom during the reception, decorate the going-away car, make sure all personal belongings are taken from the ceremony and reception sites, escort the guests to their cars, and direct guests to parking and rest-room facilities.

The honor attendant, best man, bridesmaids, and groomsmen are all responsible for purchasing their individual attire for the wedding. They are included in the ceremony's processional and recessional, and they attend both the rehearsal and the rehearsal dinner. They may also be members of the receiving line.

Getting ready for a reception *can be a complex process, but a good caterer simplifies it, preparing the meal and setting up chairs and tables. Often the caterer also orders tableware, chooses linens, and sets the table.*

HIRING PROS

If you need additional help planning the wedding, it's a good idea to call in experts. Wedding professionals can make your life a lot easier by attending meetings on your behalf, scouting out the perfect location, keeping within your budget, creating a mouthwatering menu, and hunting down flowers, decorations, and entertainment.

Many vendors in the wedding business provide a one-stop service. A florist who also plans parties can assist with the decor and planning.

Finding professionals is easy. Ask for names from friends and family who have hosted successful parties, or get some referrals from your florist, stationer, reception location manager, or a reputable hotel. Many vendors in the wedding business provide a one-stop service. A florist who also plans parties, for instance, can assist with the overall decor and planning.

Leave the fine points to the experts while you concentrate on the big picture. The most called-upon professionals are the wedding coordinator or consultant, entertainment consultant, hotel wedding consultant, florist, caterer, and stationer.

Wedding consultants can do as much or as little as you wish them to—from helping out with referrals and ideas at the beginning to handling the entire affair. A consultant is an invaluable resource for arranging an out-of-town wedding, obtaining discounts, or ensuring that the other vendors give you what you want. After all,

vendors are always most eager to please a professional who may be able to offer them more work in the future.

Caterers provide delicious, beautifully presented food and capable, gracious staff to serve it. Some caterers offer full-service party planning—from the entertainment and decor to meal and bar services, equipment rentals, and staffing—a complete production on wheels. Whether you want a casual country feeling or a formal dinner with white-gloved waiters, your caterer should be able to enhance your reception while respecting your budget.

Entertainment consultants specialize in selecting music and booking performers. Although their main function is to provide music that is appropriate to the style of your wedding, they sometimes offer full-service wedding coordination as well. Your site manager might be a good source for identifying this consultant.

When putting together your wedding team, choose the vendors you feel the most

If your budget *doesn't allow the full services of a caterer, identify tasks you can afford. For example, have the caterer prepare the meal and then set up a self-service buffet.*

comfortable with, and make sure all of the bases are covered (see page 35). In dealing with these professionals, you should:

- CONTACT THE VENDOR'S REFERENCES TO CONFIRM THAT PREVIOUS CLIENTS WERE SATISFIED WITH THEIR SERVICE

- AGREE ON A BACKUP PLAN WITH EACH VENDOR IN CASE OF BAD WEATHER OR OTHER UNFORESEEN PROBLEMS

- DETERMINE WHETHER THE PRICE INCLUDES GRATUITIES

Don't worry that if you hire professionals, your wedding might not be a reflection of you. Professionals pride themselves on interpreting and creatively executing your vision. Their number one priority is to research the best goods and services and then give you choices. The final decisions will always be left up to you.

Go ahead and state your requirements and preferences right up front. All of the vendors you hire should honor your ideas, budget, and style. That means they agree to work within your budget and to respect any limitations that the reception site might impose. No matter what amount of money you choose to spend, there will always be a creative way to orchestrate the wedding you envision.

REGISTRY STRATEGIES

With your combined households, the two of you may already have enough china and utensils to serve an army. To avoid duplicates (who needs three toasters?), inform family and friends about the gifts you most need and want by registering your specific preferences with stores.

Start by taking an inventory of both households. Tear out magazine and catalog pages for inspiration. Then identify the general areas you want to focus on.

New Places to Register

Looking for computer or stereo equipment instead of formal china? More couples are registering at nontraditional places such as hardware, computer, and stereo stores, garden centers, wine merchants, cooking shops, booksellers, home-improvement warehouses, and antique shops. Even some gift catalogs offer bridal registry services.

If the two of you already have plenty of casual dinnerware and flatware, consider registering for just the formal patterns. Or how about items such as candleholders and candles, slipcovers for chairs or a sofa you already own, curtain rods and curtains, bar accessories, and accent pillows for furniture that needs a little pick-me-up? Look for items such as thick, white hotel-style towels; linen napkins (specify your new initials for any embroidery); and classic duvet covers and shams. And don't forget about cookware or bathroom accessories such as toothbrush holders, makeup mirrors, soap dishes, drawer organizers, and countertop canisters.

USING STORE EXPERTS

The easiest way to locate everything on your wish list is to register at large and reputable department stores, along with a few specialty shops. Most stores that offer a bridal registry service have a consultant who will browse the store with you, providing advice and guidance. It's wise to make an appointment whenever possible. Look around by yourselves first, then ask for the consultant's assistance. Let the consultant know what unusual as well as practical things you'd like to receive.

To minimize stress, register as early as possible as a favor to those who want to purchase engagement and shower gifts. Ask the bridal party to spread the word regarding where you're registered and to include that information on shower invitations. Check the exchange and return policies of the stores where you're registering, and find out how long your registry will

Whatever you have your heart set on, include it in your registry—
even if it's a bit more offbeat than china and silverware.

stay in each store's computer. Usually the store will update it as you receive gifts or if merchandise becomes unavailable. Be sure to register gifts in many price ranges.

Keep track of the gifts you receive: Use an alphabetized log in a binder or note-

are flexible about exchanging presents. It's not necessary to tell guests you returned their gift. Thank them for the original present; if someone asks about a return, just describe the object for which you exchanged it, and explain the situation.

**Record some of your thoughts regarding the gifts you receive.
It'll be helpful when you're writing thank-you notes.**

book (see page 25), start an index-card filing system, or record the gifts in your home computer. Hold onto all tags and warranty information that come with each gift. Record pertinent information—a description of the gift, the name and address of the sender, the date the gift arrived, the store where it was purchased, any thoughts you have regarding the gift (helpful when writing thank-you notes), and when you sent your thank-you note.

Don't worry if you receive duplicate gifts. Return policies vary, but most stores

If a gift arrives damaged, contact the store it came from immediately to arrange a replacement. If you can't determine what store the present was purchased from, have your mother or honor attendant contact the guest for assistance.

Traditionally, guests have up to one year to send wedding gifts. If you think a present has been lost, the best thing to do is wait, since it simply may not have been sent yet. If a guest sent a gift and did not receive a thank-you note, he or she may contact you to confirm receipt.

It's Party Time

---　✴　---

GET READY FOR A FLURRY OF COCKTAIL PARTIES, SHOWERS, BRUNCHES, TEAS, AND OTHER FESTIVITIES AS FAMILY AND FRIENDS COME TOGETHER TO CELEBRATE YOUR UPCOMING MARRIAGE. ENJOY THE ATTENTION YOU'LL GET!

Unlike parties of the past, today's prewedding get-togethers can be anything from a luxurious day at a health spa to an exciting day at the ballpark. And wedding showers are no longer for women only; in fact, the coed variety has become increasingly popular in recent years.

Coworkers, friends, family, or anyone in the wedding party can throw a shower in your honor. Sometimes you'll attend several. Here are fun ideas for wedding showers. The host may:

◆ SELECT A SPECIFIC ROOM OF THE HOUSE AND ASK THAT EACH GUEST BRING A GIFT FOR THAT ROOM

◆ ASK THAT GUESTS BRING MUSIC, CONCERT TICKETS, OR OTHER ENTERTAINMENT-RELATED GIFTS

◆ MAKE THE HONEYMOON DESTINATION THE THEME; GIFTS CAN BE BEACH ESSENTIALS, WINE, OR TOUR BOOKS

A tradition that dates to the fifth century, the bachelor party lets the groom celebrate his last night as a single guy. The party might be hosted by the best man, the groomsmen, or a close friend. No longer the requisite striptease bash, this rite of passage can be as simple as the gang going to a sporting event or smoking cigars and playing cards at a men's club. Camaraderie is the best part of the event.

For a bachelorette party, you might be whisked away for a day of wine tasting, to a fancy restaurant for a gourmet meal, to a girls-only barbecue, or to a hotel suite rented just for massages. Whatever the venue, bask in the attention and enjoy the company of your friends and family.

If you're hosting your own prewedding get-together, give yourself a break

After the first few wedding parties,
you may be ready for a rest.

by keeping the party simple. Family and friends are the most important ingredients. You might just want to invite your wedding party over for an informal working lunch or dinner designed to discuss the planning and to help you organize. Party members can keep you posted on their progress and take on new tasks if they're ready for more. Don't bother with a complicated menu or decorations for this sort of gathering; just order take-out food for a quick buffet.

A perfect party and gift combination for the bridesmaids is to treat them (and yourself, of course) to a relaxing day at a spa. There you'll all be pampered with facials and hair treatments, therapeutic mud or herbal baths, and spa cuisine. If your budget doesn't allow for splurging at a traditional spa, reserve time at a salon, or host a day of pampering at your home.

Last Call for Parties

Ask your friends and family not to hold any parties during the last week or two before the wedding. That way the bride and groom will have time to deal with all the last-minute wedding details without feeling pressured and stressed-out by more parties.

Wherever you hold the party, it offers a relaxed way for attendants from out-of-town to meet everyone else participating in the ceremony. Surround yourself with a few close friends or family members for a simple breakfast the day of your wedding. Distract yourself from the inevitable stress by chatting and enjoying the food.

SIMPLE SOLUTIONS

HOSTING YOUR OWN DINNER

Sometimes you may need to organize a prewedding get-together yourself, whether it's the rehearsal dinner, a thank-you to the attendants, or the first time the families of the bride and groom meet each other.

Simple

Cook a one-pot meal, such as lasagna, chili, stew, or paella. Then make salad from bagged, prewashed lettuce. Add a crusty round of bread, wine, a store-bought fruit tart, and you're done.

Simpler

Many top restaurants have couriers who deliver complete meals. Try pasta and sauce from an Italian trattoria, or exotic entrées from a Thai restaurant. Serve the meal on your own dishware.

Simplest

Take your guests out to a restaurant. It needn't be expensive— every community has its bargain spots. Liquor makes the bill rise quickly, so serve cocktails at home first.

STEPS to take Now

——✳——

1 Set the date based on the **season** that best suits the type of wedding you envision. **2** If you are planning to use a specific **florist or caterer,** check with that service provider and then select a date based on his or her schedule. **3** Consider your **lifestyle** and the atmosphere in which your guests will be most comfortable and relaxed. **4** Assemble a three-ring **binder to keep track** of all wedding-related data according to category. **5** Use **master lists** to stay organized: Create a contact list with everyone's phone numbers for quick reference. Come up with a to-do list and **delegate responsibilities** to the wedding party and any professionals you hire. **6** When dealing with vendors, be sure to **obtain a contract** or written agreement from each professional providing a service or product. That way there won't be any last-minute surprises. **7** Decide on a realistic budget and stick to it. Use **diplomacy** when figuring out who will be paying for what. **8** Don't forget the **legal details,** such as marriage-license requirements, name changes, and prenuptial agreements. ●

FIRST THINGS FIRST

LAYING THE FOUNDATION

* —— * —— *

It's time to begin mapping out exactly what you want, from the time of year you'll tie the knot to the location of your wedding and the style of your gown. Since most couples don't have a limitless budget, the challenge is to figure out which elements are essential and which you can forgo.

Find creative ways to include what really matters to both of you. For instance, if your budget is tight but you have your heart set on an ultraformal white-tie-and-tails ball, pare down your guest list and go all out for a more intimate group. On the other hand, if you can't imagine a celebration without all your relatives and friends taking part, opt for an informal wedding that allows you to entertain more guests. Placing what's important to you at the top of the priority list is what makes the celebration uniquely yours.

A lovely wedding need not be complicated. Plan a stress-free event that fulfills your dreams without driving you crazy.

SETTING THE DATE

※

J UNE IS THE MOST POPULAR MONTH FOR WEDDINGS, BUT DON'T FEEL BOUND
TO FOLLOW THE CROWD. THERE MAY BE A DAY THAT HOLDS SPECIAL SIGNIFI-
CANCE FOR YOU, SUCH AS THE DATE THE TWO OF YOU MET OR BECAME ENGAGED.

The Victorians believed that the luckiest day on which to marry was the groom's birthday. But for some types of weddings, June is ideal—especially if mild weather is important to the event. Garden weddings, for instance, are often best in late spring or early summer, when the landscape and colors are at their peak. An almanac or the weather service can advise you on whether the date you are considering is suited to an outdoor affair in your area.

Availability is also a factor in choosing a date. Many wedding professionals and locations—including churches and synagogues—are booked well in advance, so inquire right away. June is the most popular month, followed by August, July, May, September, October, April, and December. As for days of the week, Saturdays in particular fill up early. Sometimes a vendor who is booked solid for Saturday may be

The average wedding requires six months to plan, but you can probably pull off a small, informal wedding in as little as three months.

willing to negotiate a lower fee in exchange for your accepting a different day. If you have your heart set on a specific caterer, florist, or musician, check with that service provider first and select a date based on his or her schedule.

Involve your wedding team in your plans
and delegate as many tasks as possible.

When narrowing down your date options, ask relatives, friends, and members of the wedding party for any potential conflicts. Don't forget to check with your employer about scheduling time off. Also, take a look at a calendar of upcoming events in your area for anything that could wreak havoc with your plans.

Getting married on a holiday can offer your guests a minivacation and a delightful event all in one. But beware of booking and transportation problems. If you decide to have your wedding on a holiday, plan well in advance to beat the congestion.

FULL SPEED AHEAD

Staying organized is the key to planning a stress-free wedding. The first bit of advice may sound unnecessary, but you'll find it a godsend: Set up a three-ring binder to keep track of every bit of wedding-related data. Use dividers to separate the binder into categories: contact list, schedule, budget, location, decor, entertainment, guest lists, catering, gifts, prewedding parties, attire, ceremony, reception, and honeymoon. Include plenty of blank paper for notes, sketches, and to-do lists. Whenever you receive any paperwork or samples—such as a swatch, a picture, or a contract—punch holes in it and immediately file it in its corresponding section.

With your binder in hand, you can start thinking about the location and style of your ceremony and reception. Look through bridal magazines and catalogs for bridal gowns, bridesmaids' dresses, and groom's and groomsmen's attire. Start collecting information on professionals you

may want to hire—wedding consultant, florist, caterer, photographer, videographer, musicians. Begin composing your guest list and ask both sets of parents to do the same. Think about the budget. How much can you afford to spend on your wedding? Will parents be contributing?

The average wedding requires about six months to plan (see pages 138–139 for a sample planning schedule), so be sure to leave enough time. The more intimate the gathering, the shorter the planning period you can get away with. You can probably pull off a small, informal wedding in as little as three months. You will need to order your gown as soon as possible, however, since it can take months to arrive.

The Right Time for a Honeymoon

If you'll be embarking on your honeymoon right after the event, think about how your destination meshes with your wedding date. Hurricane season in the Caribbean won't make for happy memories. And though a winter wedding gives you the perfect opportunity to ski through your honeymoon, a major snowstorm could put a crimp in your travel plans. Of course, you could opt to have your wedding when it works best and delay the honeymoon until a better time.

If your heart *is set on getting married in a picturesque location, call at once. Its availability may determine your wedding date.*

If you know you're a procrastinator or if your wedding date is fast approaching, consider a full-service location such as a hotel or country club. Such facilities are usually prepared to pull together intimate or large affairs on short notice.

A consultant can free up your time by coordinating the tasks that require special expertise. That leaves you free to focus on the details you're most excited about, such as picking out your wardrobe and choosing members of the wedding party.

USING MASTER LISTS

Two organizational tools make it much easier to coordinate planning tasks—a contact list and a to-do list.

Creating a contact list is easy. Break down the categories of phone numbers you'd like to keep on file: wedding party, family members, gift registries, vendors,

locations, and wedding consultants. You may already have relatives' and friends' phone numbers in an address book, but it's beneficial to keep all of them on your contact list for quick reference. Add vendors and consultants to your list as you go. Whenever possible, include pager, fax, and cell phone numbers—you never know when you'll need to reach somebody right away. You can keep your list on the computer for easy updating, but be sure to print it and carry it in your binder. To save time, update the list whenever you've made significant changes, and move the most-used telephone numbers to the top.

When people ask, "What can I do to help?" it's great to have a master to-do list at your fingertips. It should list all the tasks that need doing, organized by category. When someone offers assistance, refer to your list and the category where that person's skills would be most helpful. If your honor attendant is a fabulous shopper, let her help find the bridesmaids' dresses—or at least narrow down the choices. If the best man knows how to set up a bar, ask him to help with the liquor order. If a bridesmaid has perfect penmanship, have her address envelopes and make out place cards. Hand everyone in the wedding party his or her own to-do list. Then give vendors specific lists with their duties. As jobs are completed or as new ones come up, update the master to-do list accordingly.

As project manager, you will probably have the longest to-do list of all. To make your list more manageable, break it down into smaller categories that you can tackle one at a time. Break down the categories again if they still seem too cumbersome. When you have a more manageable list in hand, find additional friends, relatives, or neighbors who wouldn't mind helping you with some small task. Perhaps a neighbor has some extra chairs you can borrow, or a friend has some beautiful platters she wouldn't mind lending. Keep tabs on who is helping you and how they're contributing. This will come in handy when you sit down to write thank-you notes.

You won't have to manage those tasks you've delegated to vendors. These people have plenty of experience in their fields, so no hand-holding should be required. If anything, they'll hold your hand.

KEEPING TABS

From time to time, though, do check in with vendors to make sure that they are taking care of everything and that all tasks remain on track. Check in frequently as well with your team of volunteers. If time is becoming tight and your list of to-do's

The Bottom Line on Flowers

When setting a wedding date, keep in mind that flowers are more costly out of season and around Valentine's Day and Mother's Day. To avoid paying an arm and a leg, choose flowers that are in season at the time of your wedding and, if it's at all possible, steer clear of these holiday times.

is still quite long, ask your friends and family for more help. They can always say no, but they probably won't. Or, if your budget can stand it, assign some of the must-do tasks to a professional helper.

A master to-do list *is an indispensable tool in helping you keep track of the numerous details that contribute to making your day perfect.*

SETTING THE TONE

---✳---

N O TWO WEDDINGS ARE EVER THE SAME, SINCE EACH COUPLE BRINGS THEIR OWN SPECIAL CHARM WITH THEM. THE MOST MEMORABLE WEDDINGS ARE THOSE THAT CAPTURE THE ESSENCE OF THE BRIDE AND GROOM.

Weddings range from the informal to the very formal. In deciding what you want, let the ceremony set the tone for the celebration. A wedding that takes place before 200 guests in a cathedral would call for a formal reception, whereas a small service in a quaint chapel could be followed by a home reception. Here's a guide to the four degrees of formality:

Informal. Although this may suggest barefoot nuptials at the beach or a picnic at a rustic farmstead, an informal wedding needn't be any less traditional than a formal affair. Indeed, informal weddings have a long history: Before the 20th century, most ceremonies or receptions were held at the home of the bride's parents. And an informal wedding is not necessarily small —it can be as large as your budget and the setting allow. Any number of bridesmaids and groomsmen is fitting, as is any type of meal service. Usually, simple and unaffected attire is the order of the day, as are handwritten invitations and a warm family atmosphere.

Semiformal. This style is a blending of formal and informal elements—perfect if you have a large guest list but don't want

---

SIMPLE SOLUTIONS

INFORMAL WEDDINGS

N OT EVERYONE DESIRES OR CAN AFFORD a large, formal wedding. The best wedding is one that reflects your personality and style and is relaxing for all involved. Here are some simple alternatives to a formal wedding that are both satisfying and memorable.

Simple

An at-home wedding. Getting married at your home or that of a relative makes for a wonderful, intimate feeling. Choose the backyard, under a gazebo, by the swimming pool, or in the living room.

Simpler

A private ceremony in a judge's chambers. It could be just the two of you and two witnesses. Follow the marriage ceremony with a reception and invite only close friends and family.

Simplest

A surprise wedding. Invite family and friends to a cocktail party. Announce your intentions and astonish everyone by introducing the officiant and then exchanging vows.

Whatever theme you choose, your wedding should reflect your personal style.

an elaborate setting or meal service. If engraved invitations appeal to you, then use them—but you could enclose in each envelope a decidedly informal scattering of pressed wildflowers. The bride can wear a long satin gown, as at a formal wedding, but with a less formal shoulder-length veil. Meal service can combine hors d'oeuvres on trays, a buffet, and a sit-down service.

Very formal. The bride at a very formal wedding wears a full-length gown, plus a cathedral-length train and veil. Guests arrive in their most elegant attire. The wedding party usually includes a flower girl and a ring bearer. Pages may carry the train down the aisle. Invitations are engraved, the guest list is large, and a live orchestra provides the entertainment.

Live music, glorious flowers, and beautiful place settings round out the picture at a formal wedding. Guests dress in tuxedos and gowns.

Formal. Such celebrations naturally lend themselves to large guest lists, engraved or hand-lettered invitations, and an elegant sit-down meal service with many courses. The bridal party wears formal attire. Live music, glorious flowers, and beautiful place settings round out the picture. A formal wedding also provides guests with a marvelous opportunity to get dressed up in tuxedos and gowns.

After a cocktail hour, multiple courses are served by white-gloved waiters.

Although certain locations are suited to a particular style of wedding, many sites can accommodate any style of celebration. A hotel's ballroom becomes the perfect setting for an intimate family affair once partitions are moved into place. For an interesting twist, choose a casual setting for a formal wedding.

THEMES AND VARIATIONS

---✳---

THE THEME AND STYLE OF YOUR CELEBRATION come through in the decor, attire, ambience, and ceremonial flourishes that you choose. The fun part is finding the elements that best represent your vision. Whatever you decide on—even if you borrow a theme—your celebration will be unique. At no other time will the same mix of people gather at the same location in a manner specifically designed by you.

The Holiday Wedding. A wedding held during the Christmas season—replete with holly and poinsettias, festive carolers, a gown made of velvet, and family and friends—is an occasion few could ever forget. An Easter-season wedding invokes visions of beautiful pastel dresses, soft-hued flowers, colored eggs, and a parade of wide-brimmed bonnets. Or get married on Valentine's Day, surrounded by hearts, roses, and chocolates.

The Candlelit Wedding. Try this romantic idea for an evening celebration. The wedding party walks down the aisle carrying candles; guests can hold candles as well. Line the aisle with pillar candle torchères. At the reception, numerous candles of varying sizes cast their flickering light on the guest tables and also illuminate the walkways.

The Destination, or Honeymoon, Wedding. Hold the wedding at your honeymoon destination. As soon as the wedding is over, you're on your vacation! The best part of the honeymoon wedding is that everyone gets to enjoy the destination along with the happy couple.

The Long-Weekend Wedding. When guests will be traveling to the wedding from far and wide, you may want to plan a weekend full of opportunities for everyone to get together. Friends and relatives can help plan barbecues, picnics, and touch football, softball, and other games in a nearby park.

The Renaissance Wedding. With costumes rich in warm gold tones and deep burgundy hues, this period theme is perfect for a fall or winter wedding. The bride and her attendants wear velvet and brocade designs; the invitations are written on scrolls; and the music features mandolins, harpsichords and lyres. Wrought-iron candelabras and ivory-colored candles complete this romantic theme.

The Nautical Wedding. The classic color scheme of navy blue, ivory, and yellow accents this celebration, usually held on a boat or at a seaside location. Print the wedding invitations in navy ink on ivory stock. The groom and his groomsmen wear navy blazers and ivory slacks. Serve seafood, highlighted by the catch of the day, and finish with a pale-blue cake adorned with seashells and other nautical motifs. Silver bos'n's whistles, engraved with the wedding date, make great party favors.

The Military Wedding. If either the bride or groom is in the service, then having a military wedding is a wonderful way to honor the two of them. The military member can wear a full-dress uniform. Choose locations relating to the military, such as the chapel at a military academy or post. Trim invitations with gold braid or accent each one with a crest or other military adornment. At the close of the ceremony, highlight the recession with a dramatic arch of steel—an honor guard holding sabers or swords above the newlyweds' path.

A very formal wedding held at the beach is almost irresistible. Or you might want to pick an elegant setting, like a museum or gallery, for an informal affair.

The time of day slightly affects the degree of formality, mostly in terms of attire. As a rule, weddings at high noon or in the evening are considered more formal.

DEFINING QUESTIONS

Still unsure about what tone to choose? Use these questions to clarify the different ideas you are considering:

Should you have a formal or an informal wedding? If you envision an elaborate celebration with an extensive meal service, then what you want is a formal wedding. If you desire a more casual atmosphere full of mingling and plenty of dancing, then the wedding you want is less formal.

Do you prefer a religious ceremony or a civil one? Decide whether to get married in a place of worship, at city hall, or in some other location. If you're marrying in a place of worship that is new to you, ask about special requirements. Sometimes premarital counseling is a prerequisite.

Do you want a traditional or a non-traditional ceremony? Is it important for you to follow rituals passed down from generation to generation, or do you see yourselves forging new paths and following your own rules? Would a mix of both be best? If so, which traditions do you feel most strongly about including, and which would you like to change?

The bottom line is that the simplest wedding for you to orchestrate on your own is an informal, intimate gathering. The level of complexity climbs with the guest count and degree of formality.

Destination weddings *are easy. Hotels and resorts offer special packages for you and your guests. Just pick one, show up, and enjoy!*

Don't let these facts deter you if a formal wedding is what you really want. Just be realistic about the amount of time and energy it will take to pull it off.

A REALISTIC BUDGET

Times have changed. No longer does the bride's family always foot the bill for her entire wedding. One popular arrangement is for the couple, the bride's family, and the groom's family each to pay one-third. Or, the couple takes full responsibility for expenses, and their parents contribute whatever they can in the form of a gift rather than an obligation. Or, after calculating a per-person cost, each family can pay for its own guests.

Always use diplomacy when figuring out who is paying. Decide whether you want to be together when you approach your parents about financial arrangements, or whether it would be more comfortable for each of you to discuss the matter with your own set of parents.

If you decide to stick with the traditional approach of having the bride's family pay for most of the expenses, here's how it typically breaks down:

The bride's family. They pay for the engagement party, invitations and thank-you notes, ceremony costs (except for the officiant's fee), the wedding consultant,

Whether your budget is $4,000 or $40,000, there are numerous smart ways to get the most for your money.

the reception, the photographer, the videographer, the bride's attire, the corsages and boutonnieres for the bride's family, flowers for the bridesmaids and flower girl, and transportation for the bridal party to the ceremony and reception.

The groom's family. They pay for the rehearsal dinner party, travel and accommodations for the groom's family, their

You can stay within budget. Prioritize what's important to you, and eliminate or tone down elements that aren't crucial.

own corsages and boutonnieres, and wedding attire for the groom and groomsmen.

The bride. She pays for the groom's wedding band, her wedding gift to the groom, her own personal stationery, gifts for her attendants, her medical exam or blood test (if either is required), and any accommodations for her attendants.

The groom. He pays for the bride's engagement ring and wedding band, his wedding gift to the bride, his own personal stationery, gifts for the best man and groomsmen, his own attire, the marriage license, his medical tests (if needed), the bride's bouquet, the officiant's fee, accommodations for groomsmen and the best man, transportation to the honeymoon, and all the honeymoon costs.

Whether the two of you are paying for your wedding or it's a collective effort between your families, decide on a budget and stick to it. There are many ways to calculate a budget, but here's the simplest:

- ◆ 50% FOR RECEPTION LOCATION, RENTALS, FOOD, BEVERAGES
- ◆ 10% FOR FLOWERS AND DECOR
- ◆ 10% FOR ENTERTAINMENT
- ◆ 10% FOR PHOTOGRAPHY AND VIDEOGRAPHY
- ◆ 10% FOR THE BRIDE'S AND GROOM'S ATTIRE
- ◆ 10% FOR FEES, INVITATIONS, TRANSPORTATION, ETC.

It doesn't hurt to ask vendors if their fees are negotiable or if there are ways to trim costs. If you hire a consultant, part of his or her job is to keep within your budget.

Decide what's most important and eliminate elements that aren't crucial to

Keeping It All Straight

To stay on budget, keep track of prices quoted, deposits you make, and balances due. Try using a computer spreadsheet or budget worksheet. Update and print out the pages periodically and keep them in your binder. Eliminate any surprise charges by getting everything in writing if it relates to costs and services.

you. If an exquisite meal is at the top of your list, spend more on food and cut back elsewhere. If you have access to a wholesale flower market, use the money you save to splurge in another area.

You can keep yourself from overspending. Whether your budget is $4,000 or $40,000, there are numerous smart ways to get the most for your money. Consider offering wine and beer instead of a full bar. Serve champagne only for the toast. Rather than hosting a grandiose, sit-down evening meal, have a breakfast, brunch, or afternoon tea. Not only will you save on food, but the costs for the alcohol will be considerably lower as well. If you're determined to have a lavish wedding, trim the guest list. You'll save on food, dinnerware, linens, flowers, favors, and staff.

Although the honeymoon is not included in the formula, consider its cost when determining your budget. You will need money left over in order to go!

LEGAL NECESSITIES

---*---

WHILE YOU'RE PLANNING THE MOST ROMANTIC DAY OF YOUR LIFE, YOU STILL NEED TO CONSIDER ALL THE LEGAL DETAILS OF A MARRIAGE—THE CONTRACTS, LICENSES, CERTIFICATES, AND NAME CHANGES INVOLVED.

All are part of making your marriage official. Marriage license requirements differ from state to state and from province to province. Contact your local government office to find out where you need to apply and what documents are required. These may include a birth certificate, proof of citizenship, blood test results, a divorce decree (if you or your spouse-to-be is divorced), or a death certificate (if either of you is widowed). Ask how long your license will be valid and what the fee is. Since both of you have to be present to apply for the license, why not go to lunch afterward to celebrate the occasion?

The marriage certificate is provided by the officiant and signed after the ceremony by the bride, groom, and two witnesses (usually the bride's honor attendant and the best man). The officiant files the document with the proper authorities; you'll receive an original certificate by mail.

DEALING WITH DETAILS

Whether you change your last name or keep your maiden name is a personal choice. Some brides keep their maiden name for professional use and adopt their husband's name socially. Many brides hyphenate their maiden name and new last name or use their maiden name as

Finalize *all the legal details before the big day. That way you'll be relaxed instead of preoccupied as you walk down the aisle.*

their middle name and add on their husband's last name. If you decide to change your name, make a list of the documents you will need to revise, and check off your entries as you make the requests.

If one of you will be moving into the other's home or if you're both moving to a new home, send change-of-address cards to your friends, relatives, and anyone with whom you conduct business.

Talk openly about a prenuptial agreement. If you decide you need one, then each party should be represented by separate counsel.

Some couples have a prenuptial agreement drawn up to specify how their assets will be divided in the event of a divorce. Some prenuptial agreements also outline what sort of lifestyle each party expects during the marriage, such as whether children are expected, how finances will be handled, and how the household will be managed. Talk openly about a prenuptial agreement and discuss its objectives. If you decide you need one, then each party should be represented by separate counsel.

COVERING YOURSELVES

When dealing with vendors, be sure to obtain a contract or written agreement from each professional who is providing you with a service or product. This will eliminate any gray areas or hidden costs. The contracts can include specifics, such as how many breaks the band gets and when they can take them. No detail is too

small to include in the contract or agreement. Specify the nitty-gritty now to head off problems later. Make deposits using your credit card so that you'll have some recourse if you need to resolve a dispute.

Concerned about insurance? Request that each vendor provide you with proof of liability insurance. This relieves you of liability should one of the vendor's employees get hurt or cause an accident. Vendors may also need to carry workers' compensation insurance. If the ceremony will be at your home, contact your insurance company to confirm that you are covered for the event, should an accident occur.

Taking care of all these details early will put your mind at ease and let you breeze through the rest of the planning.

SIMPLY PUT...

ATTORNEYS' TERMS DEMYSTIFIED

liability • Responsibility for something in case of mishap. For example, your vendors should be liable for the timely delivery of goods and services.

prenuptial agreement
A contract that specifies how the bride and groom will handle their finances once married and how they'll divide their assets in the event of a divorce.

postnuptial agreement
This contract is similar to a prenuptial agreement, except that it is entered into after the marriage has taken place rather than before.

DIVE into
the Details

—✳—

1 When you shop for **wedding attire,** take along your honor attendant, your mother, or a friend for support. **2** If you can't get your **mother's gown** altered for you, carry a piece of her gown with you by incorporating some of its lace, trim, or panels into your new gown. **3** The groom should **stand out** from his groomsmen. If they wear cummerbunds, he could wear a vest. **4** Today **bridesmaids' dresses** are meant to be worn again. Shifts, chiffons, and the classic black dress are all appropriate. **5** Prepare the **guest list.** Have the bride's and the groom's families each choose half the guests, or divide the list among the bride and groom and the two families. **6** To **save money** and time, order all your stationery at once: invitations, reply cards, and thank-you notes. **7** Write your wedding **invitations** by hand if you are having a small wedding or are watching your budget. **8** **Keep a list** of those you want to thank with gifts. Then, whenever you're at a store or looking through a catalog, keep an eye out for appropriate presents. ●

DRESS, GUESTS, AND INVITES

PLANNING THE NEXT STEPS

* —— * —— *

The recipe for a wonderful wedding includes a savory mix of ingredients: charming invitations, lovely attire, gifts to express your appreciation, and the magic of having your closest friends and family there to celebrate with you.

Your invitations kick off the anticipation and set the tone for what is to come. When you set out to compile your guest list, include the people who really matter to you. Don't fret about whether they'll all blend together and mix cordially. Of course they will. It's their way of showing appreciation for being invited to participate in such a special day.

Guests will also enjoy the chance to "ooh" and "aah" at the bridal party's attire. The dresses and menswear that you choose should enhance the atmosphere of the affair.

Give gifts for the support you've received throughout the engagement. Keep the gifts simple and thoughtful to thank friends and family who helped make your day a success.

CHOOSING THE WEDDING ATTIRE

---✳---

ROMANTIC VERSUS CLASSIC, BALL GOWN VERSUS SHEATH—BRIDAL FASHIONS GO IN AND OUT OF FAVOR. BUT THERE'S NO NEED TO CONCERN YOURSELF WITH WHAT RUNWAY MODELS ARE WEARING THIS SEASON.

Follow your own taste and sense of style and choose a dress you like, using the tone of your wedding as a guide.

If your wedding is designed to be a very formal occasion, the perfect gown for you could be made of a variety of rich fabrics, such as satin and brocade for winter, or chiffon and silk for summer. The very formal gown has a full-length train and veil and is accented by long gloves if the gown does not have long sleeves. To adapt the ensemble to formal attire, you simply shorten the train, veil, and gloves.

Semiformal celebrations permit you more flexibility. Why not mix the formality of a full-length skirt with a flirty shoulder-length veil? Add a train and a headpiece, or skip them if you prefer. It's up to you.

Informal weddings allow the most variety: Stylish suits and chic slip dresses are two of the options. Of course, there's no rule against a full-length gown for an informal wedding. Just keep the lines simple and the accessories to a minimum.

If you decide to go the less-traditional route, check out evening-wear boutiques

New options in men's wedding attire let
a man express his unique personality.

or department stores for your dress. White became popular as the color for bridal wear only around 1840, when Queen Victoria chose the color for her wedding. Prior to that, brides wore a rainbow of colors. So feel free to march down the aisle in pale green, blue, yellow, soft gray, or earth tones if that's what you look best in. No matter what style you choose, if you're getting married in a place of worship, ask if it has guidelines for attire.

BRIDAL SALONS

You'll find the widest selection of dresses at a bridal salon. Ask friends, family, colleagues, florists, or your bridal consultant for referrals, then make appointments to visit a few salons. Take particular note of the service you receive and how the gowns

Choose the gown color you look best in. White became popular for brides only when Queen Victoria chose it for her wedding.

are handled—that's a good indication of how they'll handle your gown. Finally, ask to see a sample of their alteration work before deciding on a shop.

Involve your attendants when selecting your dress. Ask your honor attendant to accompany you to the bridal salon for a demonstration on how to wear the bustle and arrange the veil. Ask the salesperson whether your gown will require pressing on your wedding day, or whether you can just hang it up a few days beforehand to let the wrinkles fall out.

IT'S THE SMALL THINGS THAT SHOW YOUR FLAIR AND PUT AN INDIVIDUAL STAMP ON YOUR WEDDING.

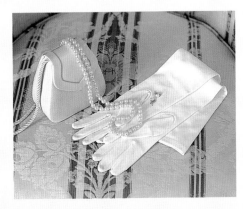

Exquisite details

Accessories will enhance your attire. Search out family treasures, chic chokers, or elegant strands of pearls. Wear long gloves if the occasion is formal. Keep essentials (lipstick and powder) in a small silk or satin purse. Avoid other accessories. The beauty of your gown and your happy smile are all you need.

Good-luck charms

A lasting wedding-day tradition, these items are talismans few brides would marry without. "Something old" represents your past: family jewelry, part of an heirloom gown, or grandmother's handkerchief. "Something new" symbolizes hope for the future: a gift from the groom, new jewelry, or lingerie. "Something borrowed" is usually an item on loan from a close, happily married friend: a veil or earrings. "Something blue"—the color of loyalty—could be a pale-blue ribbon tied to the inside of your gown.

Comfortable shoes

Where footwear is concerned, comfort is a priority. Consider purchasing your shoes a half size too large, then adding pads you can remove if your feet swell during the day. Steer clear of leather pumps. Go for satin sling-backs, mules, or square heels instead.

Match the style *of your gown to the level of formality you've chosen. Informal weddings allow for the most variety. To set just the tone you want, you can start with a simple gown and add a train, a headpiece, or gloves.*

Have a bridesmaid organize an emergency kit with supplies to handle any problems you may encounter with your attire. The kit should include safety pins, scissors for stray threads, a needle and properly colored thread for small tears, clear nail polish to repair runs in your hosiery, and white or ivory chalk to cover stains.

ORDERING THE GOWN

If your gown is being made to order, it can take anywhere from six weeks to six months to arrive. Don't be shocked if the salon expects you to pay a 50 percent non-refundable deposit (for your protection, put this on your credit card so you can challenge the fee if there's a problem).

Most salons will perform any necessary fittings and adjustments at no extra charge to ensure your gown fits perfectly. Design alterations—changing the sleeves, adding beading—are charged on a per-job basis and can be quite expensive.

Not every bride is in the market for a new gown. Maybe you've always dreamed of walking down the aisle in your mother's or grandmother's wedding dress. Have an experienced seamstress repair or refit the dress well in advance, but don't despair if that family heirloom can't be adjusted to fit you. You can still carry the past with you by salvaging some of its lace, beading, trim, or decorative panels and incorporating them into your new gown.

If you want to wear an antique gown but don't have one available from your own family, vintage boutiques often carry one-of-a-kind bridal gowns or dressy dresses that work wonderfully for a wedding. Also, secondhand stores can yield some terrific finds for brides on a tight budget.

MEN'S CHOICES

In the past, the groom and his men had few fashion choices, but like most other wedding rules, that's all changed. As the options for men's wedding attire widen, so, too, do the opportunities to express your fashion personality. Many formal-wear rental shops offer a range of suits, tuxedos, tails, and ties. To make your life easy, look around for national chains that computerize your selection and can fit out-of-town groomsmen in the same attire.

If you want a very formal look for a daytime wedding, go with the morning suit—gray cutaway jacket and gray waist-coat, with striped trousers. If you like, try jazzing it up with a tie and a white wing-collar shirt instead of the traditional ascot. In the evening, a very formal wedding calls for white tie and tails. The height of elegance, this ensemble consists of a black tailcoat, black trousers, white piqué bow

> **The options for men's wedding attire have increased greatly: You can go from white tie and tails to a Mandarin collar without a tie.**

tie, a white wing-collar shirt, and vest. Formal weddings usually mean tuxedos—black or ivory dinner jacket and trousers with a satin or grosgrain stripe hiding the outer seam. Cummerbunds are worn with single-breasted jackets to hide the waist-band while the jacket is open. Suspenders instead of belts hold up the pants. The groom should stand out from his grooms-men. If they're all wearing cummerbunds, the groom could wear a vest.

One classic look for an informal summer wedding is a navy blazer and ivory trousers. In winter, ask each groomsman to wear a dark suit; as a gift, you might provide them with matching ties. The groom can set himself apart by wearing a different tie or sporting a pocket square of a different color from that of his groomsmen.

MODERN OPTIONS

If you'd like to personalize the groom's attire or have it be less traditional, a few details are all it takes. A Mandarin collar

worn without a tie is a modern alternative to a traditional wing or turned-down collar. A three- or four-button tuxedo jacket worn with a silver tie is an alternative to the traditional single- or double-breasted jacket that is usually worn with a bow tie. If the groom chooses, instead, to wear a suit, the issue of formality and style can be resolved with tailoring and accessories. He could wear a classic double-breasted black four- or six-button suit and ask his groomsmen to wear single-breasted black suits. They could then coordinate by wearing the same French-cuffed shirts accented by black or colored satin ties.

Remember a few simple rules: Ties and pocket squares are not meant to

SIMPLY PUT...

WEDDING-GOWN STYLES

ballerina • Usually made of delicate fabrics such as silk or tulle, it includes layers of petticoats and stops from midcalf to just above the ankle.

ball gown • A fitted bodice with a floor-length full skirt that billows over layers of taffeta, tulle, or satin.

empire • High-waisted, it features a scoop neckline and a romantic skirt.

princess • The most popular, it is characterized by a fitted bodice and a gradually widening skirt.

sheath • A simple, body-hugging style that accentuates natural curves.

HEADGEAR FOR THE BRIDE OR HER ATTENDANTS CAN RANGE FROM THE CLASSIC TO THE NONTRADITIONAL.

Hair accessories

Tame unruly hair with a headband, pearl-studded clips, or hair picks. Be sure to wear your accessories around the house before the wedding to adjust them for comfort.

Veils

A blusher veil is worn over the face for the ceremony. The shoulder-length flyaway veil is most suitable for informal gowns or those that have details on the back. A fingertip veil has several layers, ending at your fingertips. The ballerina or waltz veil extends to the ankles. A chapel veil falls $2^{1}/_{2}$ yards (2.3m) from the headpiece, while a cathedral veil falls $3^{1}/_{2}$ yards (3.2m).

Floral hats

As an alternative to a traditional veil, wear a hat with fresh or silk flowers. It's perfect for garden or informal weddings.

match; the pleats of a cummerbund always point up; and a double-breasted tuxedo jacket is kept buttoned (so men don't have to wear a cummerbund).

Each groomsman can express his own sense of style with his choice of shoes, cuff links, studs, and tie. It's fine to wear fashionable shoes instead of the usual rented slip-ons. The most formal shoes are patent leather opera slippers; formal leather or woven loafers and oxfords are also appropriate wedding footwear.

BRIDESMAIDS' ATTIRE

The bridesmaids' attire should echo the bride's level of formality while flattering each attendant. This isn't as hard as it sounds. If there isn't one dress style that suits everyone, decide on one fabric and allow the styles to vary. Likewise, if the bridesmaids settle on identical dresses, adapt the style for junior bridesmaids.

These days, bridesmaids' dresses are meant to be worn more than once. Shifts, sheaths, chiffons, and classic black dresses are all appropriate. A few ideas to get you started: Black satin adds drama to a formal or very formal wedding. For a semiformal affair, simple butter-yellow tops paired with full skirts in gold-colored taffeta are glamorous. For an informal wedding, you might pair a shift with a straw hat.

Order the bridesmaids' dresses from the bridal salon where you order your own gown. The shop can easily coordinate the style of the bridesmaids' dresses with that of your wedding dress and sometimes will even offer you a discount when you purchase everything right there.

Remember, though, that you don't have to have bridesmaids' dresses made to order. Instead, you can buy delicate, sophisticated, ready-to-wear dresses from a department store or apparel shop. Another option is to check in factory outlets for dresses that are appropriate for bridesmaids.

You don't have to have bridesmaids' dresses made to order. Instead, buy ready-to-wear dresses from a department store or apparel shop.

If you buy from department stores, enlist the help of salespeople. Supply them with the colors, formality level, style, and price range you're after. The simplest method of all, of course, is to tell your bridesmaids the color scheme and then let them pick out their own dresses.

Children in the bridal party will appreciate simple attire that allows them to be comfortable. And you'll appreciate it, too, because they'll fidget a lot less. Flower girls will look adorable in ballerina-style dresses made of tulle, organza, or taffeta. Ballet slippers or buckled dress shoes are perfect with tights or folded lace-trimmed socks. The ring bearer can wear a satin or velvet suit, a child's tuxedo, a navy blazer and white trousers, or shorts with white kneesocks. If you're having pages, they should wear knickers with white kneesocks, black dress shoes, and a white dress shirt.

Ultimately, the right choice is whatever pleases you. As long as you like the way everything looks together, go for it.

If you really want *to keep it simple, have your bridesmaids and honor attendant wear the same color, but then let them each shop separately for dress styles of their choosing.*

THE GUEST LIST

---- ✳ ----

THE PEOPLE YOU CHOOSE TO SURROUND YOU ON YOUR WEDDING DAY ARE WHAT MAKE YOUR CELEBRATION MEMORABLE. THE MIX OF OLD FRIENDS, NEW FAMILY, AND UNIQUE PERSONALITIES ADDS CHARACTER TO THE DAY.

Deciding how many guests you want to have, whom to invite, and whom to leave out can be a real exercise in diplomacy. Typically, each family gets to invite half the guests, though often that can vary if one family lives out of town and doesn't expect many relatives to be able to attend. The list can also be split into thirds: The bride's family, the groom's family, and the couple each invite one-third of the guests. It all depends on what works best for you.

Start the list with your closest family and friends. Expand the circle, keeping in mind your budget, the location, and the ambience you want. While a grand cathedral calls for a larger guest list, a wedding at home usually dictates a much smaller one. Keep a list of those you would like to invite but don't have room for. As people send you their regrets (expect that perhaps 25 percent of the invitees will be unable to attend), mail out additional invitations. It's still correct if guests receive invitations up to two weeks before the wedding.

Track your guest list in whatever way seems easiest to you. You might use a computer or a low-tech approach: a rotary card file or index-card system, or a notebook.

Address the outer envelopes specifically to the people on your list. If you're inviting people's children, include their names on the inside envelope rather than tacking on

Generating the guest list can be
an exercise in crowd control.

"and Family." It makes them feel special, and erases any doubt about who's to be included. If you're inviting a single guest without an escort, address the invitation to the guest only. To include an escort of your guest's choosing, find out the person's name and add it to the invitation rather than writing "and Guest."

KEEPING TRACK

You can keep track of your guest list with the method that seems easiest to you. Try using a computer program that keeps the names in alphabetical order. Or consider one of these low-tech approaches: a notebook with each page assigned to a letter of the alphabet, a rotary card file, or an alphabetized stack of index cards.

Record the correct name spelling and title (Ph.D., D.D.S., and so on) for each guest, along with the complete address (not abbreviated) and telephone number. Include the immediate family, the wedding party, and the officiant on your list, since all will receive invitations and be included in the guest count. And don't forget to count the bride and groom!

Some couples choose to mail invitations to a few very special "guests" as a way to solicit a keepsake reply. If you and your fiancé are Roman Catholic, for instance, you might send an invitation to the pope. It's unlikely that His Holiness will be joining you, but you will receive a beautiful papal blessing. An invitation to a president or a prime minister will likely garner a congratulatory response.

If you don't receive all your responses by the date specified, call guests to confirm. Ask your fiancé and parents to help.

SIMPLE SOLUTIONS

CONTROLLING THE GUEST LIST

OFTEN, WHAT'S INTENDED as an intimate gathering turns into an extravaganza filled with business associates and your parents' "closest" friends (whom you've never met). Diplomacy and a bit of firmness can prevent this from happening to you.

Simple

Remember, it's your day. Stake out a position that lets the two of you retain veto power over your parents' choices as to which and how many guests you ultimately invite.

Simpler

Defuse the situation with your parents by discussing from the start which guests take priority. As you receive regrets, invite the guests who were not included in the first round.

Simplest

Based on the budget for the wedding and the space of the sites, firmly establish how many guests each group—the bride's family, the groom's family, and the couple—can invite.

ELEGANT ANNOUNCEMENTS

---*---

FROM THE WEDDING INVITATION TO THE THANK-YOU NOTE, YOUR WRITTEN COMMUNICATION WITH YOUR GUESTS BRINGS FORTH THE MOOD OF THE OCCASION—AND REFLECTS YOUR LOVE AND RESPECT FOR YOUR GUESTS.

Weddings are becoming less bound by tradition and more fun, so treat yours as a time to let the real you come through. To simplify the process of selecting stationery and to save on cost, it's a good idea to order all your stationery at the same time.

It all begins with the invitation, giving guests the first hint of how the wedding will unfold. Ranging from simple to elaborate, the design possibilities are endless: A flat card trimmed in gold or silver with a monogram, an etching, or an icon at the top. Traditional folded invitations mailed in double envelopes. Simple or elegant handmade papers embedded with flowers.

Selecting Postage Stamps

The right stamps can add flair to your invitation. Ask to see a catalog at the post office. From famous people to historic scenes, florals to hearts, there is bound to be a stamp that will enhance your correspondence. To eliminate rough machine handling, request that your wedding invitations be hand canceled.

Handwritten invitations on your personal stationery. Envelopes beautifully stamped with an old-fashioned wax seal.

To select your stationery, go to a stationer, a printer, a computer calligraphy service, a department store, or—to really splurge—a top-of-the-line jeweler such as Cartier or Tiffany & Co. All should have books of sample invitations you can look through to get ideas of what you like.

CHOOSING A PROCESS

You'll encounter a wide range of prices for invitations, depending on the paper, the distinct elements (invitations, reply cards, envelopes), and the printing process you choose. Thermography is the process most often used for invitations, and it's appropriate for just about any paper. Using ink and powder, it creates slightly shiny, raised letters, with an appearance very similar to engraved letters', but is much less costly. Engraving is the most expensive and most formal process. It involves making steel or copper plates that are pressed into the paper, creating an embossed effect. Hand-lettered invitations can be pricey—albeit lovely. Computer-generated lettering that mimics calligraphy is more affordable and still produces elegant results.

The only invitation a professional cannot compete with is your handwritten

CREATIVE STATIONERY

———— ✳ ————

ON THE RUN FROM MUNDANE WEDDING INVITATIONS and programs? Stop into your local stationer or department store to investigate today's new styles. Many vendors stock innovative make-it-yourself kits. Start with beautiful papers, an image or a theme that grabs your attention, and take it from there.

Jazz up your *envelopes with store-bought adhesive wax seals, foil stickers, or rubber stamps. Sprinkle dried flowers inside.*

An imaginative *scroll makes a unique invitation. Or use the style for a wedding program. Guests can take the scroll home as a memento.*

Wedding programs *can be dressed up with monograms, bound with delicate ribbon, and placed in a basket near the entryway.*

Handwrite invitations *on preprinted cards. You can soften the effect by attaching a piece of translucent paper with a ribbon.*

one—the epitome of grace and elegance. If you have the time and inclination, then by all means write yours.

Handwritten invitations make sense if you're having a small wedding or watching your budget. Use personal stationery, or choose something unique for the occasion. A black fountain pen creates a beautiful look; use one with a squared-off nib for a

protocol, here's the rule: The phrase "the honour of your presence" is reserved for inviting guests to a place of worship; "the pleasure of your company" is used when the ceremony takes place anywhere else. If you need inspiration, look through the stylebooks of the professional stationer you choose. You'll find wording guidelines to address every style of ceremony.

If you want a less formal invitation, experiment with alternative ink colors on samples of invitation stock provided by your stationer.

more calligraphic effect. Black ink is always appropriate, but if you want a less formal invitation, experiment with alternative ink colors on samples of invitation stock provided by your stationer.

Of course, your invitation can say whatever you like. If you're a stickler for

For a sit-down *reception dinner at home, place cards and table numbers add elegance. Ask an attendant to write them for you.*

If you are acting as the hosts of your own wedding—or if you simply want to issue a more personal invitation—you can use a less traditional wording, such as "Ann and James, along with their families and friends, joyfully invite you to share in the celebration of their marriage," or even "While the events of our lives are unfolding and our dreams are being fulfilled, we joyfully invite you…"

One style note: Although it looks peculiar, dates are spelled out rather than written as numbers. This means spelling out the year as well as the time of day.

ADDRESSING GUESTS

Addressing envelopes has some rules but does not require a course in etiquette. Your stationer can give you full details, but here are some general guidelines:

Try not to use abbreviations—except for titles (Mr., Mrs., Ms., Jr., and Dr.)—anywhere on your invitations, envelopes, or other stationery. Single women and female children are addressed as Ms. or Miss; male children under the age of 13 are addressed as Master. Military, religious, and certain professional titles can be tricky, so ask your stationer for assistance.

If you use double envelopes, write out the guest's full name and address on the outer envelope. First names and addresses are not used on the inner envelope, just titles and last names. You don't have to put the names of children under 18 on the outer envelope. List them on the inner envelope under their parents' names.

Don't worry about proper address for guests who are divorced or separated. Just use the name you know them by until they inform you of a change.

Including a response card makes it easy for guests to reply. The cards can be preprinted or handwritten; they usually include the phrase "The favour of a reply is requested" for a formal wedding, or "Kindly respond by…" for semiformal and informal occasions. "Regrets Only" response cards can work for less formal

Buy a guest book *ready made from your stationer, or buy a blank book and customize it.*

occasions as well. An artistic alternative to a traditional reply card is a self-addressed, stamped postcard adorned on the front with a beautiful black-and-white photo.

If you're inviting out-of-town guests or having your wedding during a busy time, it's helpful to send a "Save the Date" card four to six months prior to the wedding, before the invitations go out. This lets guests know the date, location, and lodging information and gives them sufficient time to make all necessary arrangements. Your stationery professional will provide you with the proper wording.

Depending on the particulars of your event, you may also need to send the following with the invitation:

◆ A SCHEDULE FOR A WEEKEND OR DESTINATION WEDDING THAT WILL INCLUDE SEVERAL EVENTS

◆ A LOCAL MAP IF SOME GUESTS WILL BE COMING FROM OUT OF TOWN

◆ RECEPTION CARDS FOR GUESTS WHO ARE INVITED ONLY TO THE RECEPTION

When ordering your invitations, you should calculate the number required per couple—not per guest—then add a few

EASY, CREATIVE PLACE CARDS

———— ✳ ————

P LACE CARDS CAN HELP YOU set the tone at any wedding-related event, be it a bridal luncheon, a casual rehearsal dinner, or a sit-down dinner at a formal reception. For informal events, use an amusing, everyday object to display the guest's name. For a formal dinner, place a hand-labeled card atop each napkin.

For a holiday wedding, *turn a pinecone into an extraordinary place-card holder with gold spray paint and a pine sprig.*

Use gourmet breadsticks *as place-card holders to add a whimsical touch to an informal party. Write guests' names on paper bands.*

For a formal reception, *handwrite each name on a preprinted card. Place on a folded napkin.*

Mark the spot *with strawberries, potted daisies, or a small tree sapling. Send your guests home with this unusual party favor.*

extras for keepsakes or in case of mistakes. Order the invitations about four months ahead of time and send them out six to eight weeks before the big day.

WEDDING PROGRAMS

Purely optional, these are used to guide your guests through the ceremony and are special mementos of your wedding. If you choose to have them, they usually list the participants; the date, time, and location of the wedding; and songs or poems from the ceremony. Design the programs on a computer to save time and money. Place the programs at each guest's seat.

OTHER PRINTED ITEMS

Seating cards and table numbers assist your guests at the reception. For a simple wedding, let people sit wherever they choose—and dispense with the need for these cards. Otherwise, have them printed to implement specified seating. Seating cards direct guests to their tables and are arranged alphabetically by guest name at the entrance to the reception. A number on each table helps guests find their seats.

Thank-you notes are the finale to a grand affair, so try not to cut corners with a generic response. Write directly to each person or couple who gave you a wedding gift. Mention the item given and how you plan to use it, even if the gift was cash. Your thoughtfulness will be appreciated.

GUEST BOOKS

Yet another optional accessory for your wedding is the guest book. Guest books can be easily found at most stationery shops, department stores, and party-supply stores. Although many have lines where guests simply sign their names, you might choose one without lines so guests can write whatever they wish—ideally, a personal message. For a customized look, try a bound book. It makes a beautiful guest book and can be ordered with titles on the front and special paper inside (look in the Yellow Pages under "Bookbinders").

Display the guest book prominently where guests will be sure to see it. Place several ballpoint pens alongside the book (avoid using felt-tip pens; they run). And last, make sure you ask your bridesmaids and groomsmen to write the first entries.

Make It a Group Project

When your guest list is complete, invite your parents, the entire wedding party, and other friends (especially anyone with elegant handwriting) over to address the invitations. What could be a chore becomes fun when everyone gathers to write and chat.

THANK-YOU GIFTS

---*---

THE TOKENS OF YOUR APPRECIATION, LOVE, AND THANKS DON'T HAVE TO BE LAVISH, JUST THOUGHTFUL. TO AVOID A SHOPPING ORDEAL, KEEP HANDY A LIST OF THOSE PEOPLE YOU WANT TO REMEMBER WITH GIFTS.

Whenever you're at a store, traveling, or thumbing through a catalog, keep an eye out for presents. Antique and vintage stores are great sources for period jewelry or old-fashioned combs and brushes. These items have loads of character and are sometimes less expensive than comparable items at major department stores.

For bridesmaids, strands of pearls are a sentimental favorite. Or what about a marvelous makeup bag full of goodies that will help them prepare for the party? You might choose to give them fabulous hair clips or chic gloves. Or you can combine smaller items to create a themed package. Pair painted flower boxes with seeds and soil, or fill a decoupage box with soaps, gels, and beauty masks.

For the groomsmen, accessorize their tuxedos by giving vests with flair, chic ties, cashmere socks, novelty watches, or cuff links. A manicure set or a shoeshine kit is something your groomsmen can use before the wedding, and a beautiful flask or decanter is always popular.

Next-Morning Gifts

After the hubbub of the wedding and reception, you and your beloved need some quiet time together. Make the next morning special by exchanging gifts you've chosen for each other—especially if you're not going on a honeymoon just yet.

IDEAS FOR EVERYONE

A creative way to give presents to the children in your party is to incorporate gifts into the ceremony. If yours is an informal, outdoor ceremony, the ring bearer could pull down the aisle a wagon (holding the pillow and rings), which he gets to keep. The flower girl can follow on a tricycle. Other great, simple ideas for children's gifts might be tickets to the zoo or circus, lunch boxes filled with art supplies, a classic book, a whimsical alarm clock, or one share of stock in a toy manufacturer, fast-food chain, or theme-park company.

Many couples also give gifts to their parents in gratitude for their support and assistance. Possibilities include a blooming fruit tree in a beautiful urn, vintage desk accessories, an antique or modern Bible with a special note from you, or a piece of art in an attractively decorated frame.

Another thoughtful gift is a donation to the recipients' favorite charity made in their name. Write a personal thank-you note to the recipients and include a certificate of thanks provided by the charity.

Need help with a gift for your partner? A bride might appreciate a silver-plated engraved key to your new home, a framed love poem, a video of the groom telling her what he loves about her, flowers galore in the honeymoon suite, or heirloom jewelry. For the groom, consider special commemorative cognac with a decanter, luggage, wine that should age 10 years before it can be opened, cigars and cigar accessories, an engraved watch or clock, or scented massage oil and an IOU.

Although there is no rule determining when to offer gifts, bridesmaids' presents are traditionally given at a party held in their honor or at the rehearsal dinner. Groomsmen receive their presents at the bachelor party or rehearsal dinner. Children's gifts can be given at the rehearsal or at the rehearsal dinner. Give parents their gifts the day before the wedding, or have them delivered while you are away.

You may also want to give a token of thanks to a close friend who performed at your wedding, to hosts of prewedding parties, to any friends who hosted your out-of-town guests, or to other volunteers who made your life easier during the planning and the event. If you do not plan to give a gift, send a written thank-you.

LOOKING FOR THE PERFECT GIFTS FOR MEMBERS OF THE BRIDAL PARTY? HERE ARE SOME SIMPLE SUGGESTIONS.

Girlfriend purses

Complete your bridesmaids' ensembles by giving them pretty "girlfriend purses," which they can carry on the wedding day. Satin purses are especially appropriate. The color should complement their attire, but doesn't need to match any colors exactly.

Stylish men's accessories

For "shear" perfection, give the guys in your wedding party vintage-style shaving sets made up of a razor, brush, and shaving mug. These are great gifts even if you don't know their shaving preferences. You can usually find these items at antique stores and boutiques, or through catalogs.

SET THE Stage

—✳—

1 Pick the **right location.** Check places that have sentimental value or that you're instantly attracted to. Consider full-service locations that provide a range of services. **2** Make sure you'll be able to transport everything you need to the site with **minimum fuss.** If logistics are a problem, scratch that location. **3** Find out the **rules and restrictions** of your wedding and reception sites well ahead of time. **4** Plan the **decor** to create the scene you imagine. If plenty of ambience is built into the location, you won't have to start from the ground up. **5** Hire a florist or **delegate** floral assignments to family and friends—or use a combination of the two methods. **6** If you'll be doing the **catering** yourself, make the reception a simple affair such as an afternoon tea. **7** Add extra touches to **enhance the atmosphere:** candles, specialty linens, or childhood photos. **8** **Select the caterers** and decide how much to assign them—just menu planning, meal preparation and delivery, or the whole production. **9** **Compose a menu** that includes your favorite foods. Personalize it with a family recipe. ●

CREATING THE SCENE

MAKING YOUR WEDDING MEMORABLE

✳ —— ✳ —— ✳

Putting a wedding together is like throwing a wonderfully personal party where you and your partner are the guests of honor. Like any good party, it is a mélange of elements—guests, food, flowers, music, and decorations.

As you weigh the possibilities for a location, consider ambience as well as logistics. Once you choose a site, think about the look and feel you want to achieve, letting the location, time of year, and level of formality be your guide.

Act as a coordinator, and do only those tasks you really want to do and have time for. Hire professionals, and delegate jobs to family and friends. You will be surprised at how much support you'll get when you ask for it.

Break each task down into small, manageable steps. The specifics will fall into place effortlessly. It's a thrill to see all the careful planning come together for an event your photographer will capture—and you'll enjoy remembering for years.

CHOOSING SITES

———— ✳ ————

WHEN YOU'RE LOOKING FOR THE PERFECT LOCATION, START WITH THE PLACES FOR WHICH YOU FEEL AN AFFINITY. HAS THE PUBLIC GARDEN WITH ITS BEAUTIFUL GOLDFISH POND ALWAYS BEEN A SENTIMENTAL FAVORITE?

Would the restaurant where you or your partner popped the question provide just the right touch of romance? Maybe the familiarity of your family home offers the intimacy you want for your celebration. Think about where you'll feel comfortable. If you're having a good time and are happy and relaxed, your guests will feel good too.

Remember that the decor, food, and guests all need to find their way to the site without too much hassle. A little brainstorming will often yield a simple solution to minor logistical difficulties. If the picturesque beach you're thinking of requires a steep hike and many of your guests are

elderly, you'll need to come up with a better plan. But don't give up on the idea of a beach wedding. Instead, scout around for a restaurant on the shore, a beach club, or a cozy cove with easy access.

Or maybe you're having a small gathering at a mountaintop park, but the caterers have no way to heat the food. Sure, you could change sites, but you could also forgo a hot meal in favor of a cold buffet and enjoy the fabulous view.

If you can't think of a simple way to make a site work for you, just cross it off your list and move on. There are plenty of other great places out there.

All-Inclusive Locations

The term "all-inclusive" is very attractive. It can be a boon for your budget, but it can also mean extra hidden costs. Ask to see a breakdown. If you won't be using all of the services, ask for a discount. If they charge a fee for the location, ask that it be waived in exchange for your food and beverage business.

HOTELS AND RESORTS

For one-stop shopping, it's tough to beat hotels and resorts. They offer not only complete service but also a great variety of sites from which to choose. Most of these places will cater the meal and can offer referrals to trustworthy florists, photographers, musicians, and entertainers. Another bonus is that your out-of-town guests won't have to worry about looking for a place to stay nearby.

It's easy to emphasize the elegance of the setting or to downplay it, depending on the style of your wedding. You can create a formal or very formal affair in a hotel's grand ballroom, or take over

If you have your heart set on an outdoor wedding,
choose the month with the best weather.

a terrace or another less opulent space for a semiformal wedding. If the idea of having strangers present on the premises puts you off, seek out inns, bed-and-breakfasts, or hotels that offer secluded spaces on

choose to have separate sites, it's easiest for everyone involved if the two places are located no more than 30 minutes or so apart. Separate sites are common when the ceremony's held at a place of worship.

**If you can't think of a simple way to make a site work for you,
cross it off your list. There are plenty of other great places.**

their own property. You'll get the benefits of their experienced staff, along with all the privacy you could desire.

Another location that's hard to compete with is a family home—either yours or someone else's, perhaps your parents'. No other location can replicate the intimacy and familiarity of your own home. An informal garden theme lends itself perfectly to a home wedding.

It's up to you whether the ceremony and reception are held in the same location or in different venues. But if you do

If you're planning to hold a religious ceremony somewhere other than at your local place of worship, let your wedding's style serve as a guide. Do you envision a grand, stained-glass cathedral? Does the charm of a quaint synagogue or small, intimate chapel fit in better with your style?

Make an appointment to meet with the presiding minister or other person of faith, who can advise you of the requirements for getting married there.

When you're evaluating a prospective location—either for the ceremony or the

no embellishment, saving you time and money. A historic building or a blooming garden with fountains and statuary is already full of atmosphere. With their attractive locations, destination weddings also require minimal decor, which makes up for some of the expense of traveling. Tropical resorts, quaint inns, wineries, and yacht clubs all have plenty of natural ambience on their own.

Your very own town may be teeming with possibilities you hadn't even thought of—historic mansions, private estates, fruit orchards, rooftop gardens, college campus halls, romantic restaurants, or lakeside parks. Being on familiar territory can do wonders to bring down the stress level of the wedding.

Spring is the best time *for a garden wedding. Find out which month usually offers the most glorious color, then book your site.*

reception—estimate how much decoration you'll need to create the scene you envision. Some locations require almost

At each potential site, take note of the facilities available (make sure there are enough rest rooms to accommodate

---

SIMPLE SOLUTIONS

CHOOSING THE SPOT

LOCATION. LOCATION. LOCATION. This real-estate motto is just as applicable to planning a wedding. Finding the perfect spot is easier than you think when you know where to look and have the right resources. Here's some help to get you there.

Simple

Refer to local guidebooks to spark ideas. Often these reference books are well researched and will surprise you with great locations, including public beaches, parks, and mountain sites.

Simpler

Use travel agents. Not only are many of them familiar with all the hotels and hot spots in your local area, but they can also advise you on honeymoon spots that often double as wedding locations.

Simplest

Have a wedding at your parents' home or at the home of a willing friend or relative. You can't beat the location for creating an intimate atmosphere, and no fees or reservations are required.

your guests!). Familiarize yourself with the house rules ahead of time so that you can take them into consideration. A museum, for example, may not have any catering facilities or may forbid live music after a certain hour. Electric outlets may be in limited supply. The solutions are simple: Have your caterer bring in the necessary equipment, and schedule the festivities to conclude in time for the music curfew. Find out if a support staff is included to help with electrical requirements for the band and other setup needs.

Remember to ask about other events that have been held at your chosen site. If many weddings have taken place successfully at your location, chances are that your needs will be met.

WEATHER PRECAUTIONS

The weather will naturally be a factor in your preparations. Hot weather is simpler to prepare for than trying to arrange for portable heaters, tents, or a possible alternative location in case of bad weather. For an outdoor, warm-weather celebration, rent market umbrellas to shade your guests or simply provide paper fans and plenty of lemonade. An outdoor location that offers an indoor area where guests can escape the sun (or an unexpected shower) is ideal and will keep everybody happy.

If your marriage is not taking place during the summer, your best bet is to play it smart and plan an indoor affair.

PERMITS

Ask your location manager to advise you of all the safety guidelines and permits that are applicable for your location. For example, what is the maximum capacity allowed? And will the fire department allow you to light candles?

If you're having a wedding at home, ask local police about limitations on live music, noise ordinances, parking guidelines, and required permits. You may want to invite the neighbors if you're planning to make a lot of noise, or at least alert them so they can choose not to be home.

Find a location that reflects your style and personality.

If you're planning an outdoor wedding, *guard against summer heat and sudden downpours by choosing a location that can accommodate tents, canopies, or umbrellas.*

LIGHTING

When narrowing down your location options or going back for a second look, try to see the place during the hours you will be using it. This will help you evaluate lighting, which frequently becomes an issue if you're using a location such as a backyard or beach.

First you should assess the main facilities that your guests will be using, such as the rest rooms and parking and the paths to these areas. Is there sufficient existing light so that guests can find the entrance to your reception and easily negotiate any staircases? Most locations that handle special events will have plenty of light, but some areas, such as your backyard, may not be well outfitted for large groups.

If the lighting is too dim, line outdoor paths and entrances with bamboo torches or small votive candles in glass holders (both sold at party-supply stores).

If you need extensive all-around light, call in the professionals. It's best to ask your caterer, florist, or bridal consultant to take care of this kind of work. Alternatively, you can call a lighting company and get a professional quote—you certainly don't want to be responsible for understanding the power requirements or renting generators. To find a lighting company, check the phone book or ask vendors for referrals.

If the lighting is too dim, line outdoor paths and entrances with bamboo torches or small votive candles in glass holders.

Never fear; rented lighting will not ruin the mood. To the contrary: It actually adds ambience and helps your guests look great. Keep in mind that the color of the light is key. Instead of unflattering white light, ask for amber or pink. Usually a couple of strategically placed light poles do the trick. You can highlight individual tables with small candles.

WORKING WITH FLOWERS

———— ✳ ————

ONCE YOU'VE DECIDED ON A SITE, IT'S TIME TO PERSONALIZE IT FOR YOUR WEDDING. FLOWERS ARE SYNONYMOUS WITH ATMOSPHERE, AND HIRING A FLORIST IS THE EASY WAY TO ENSURE THAT EVERYTHING LOOKS JUST PERFECT.

You can also recruit talented friends and relatives to do some or all of the flowers for your wedding. Think about how much participation you want to have in the floral scheme. For the sake of simplicity, coordinate the action; don't try to lead it.

HIRING A FLORIST

A florist can create beautiful table centerpieces, the bridal bouquet, corsages and boutonnieres, and pieces for general decor such as very large arrangements and floral arches. Some florists are willing to work closely with clients; others prefer a take-charge approach and want to handle all the details themselves. Decide which personality type works best for you.

In either case, a florist who also has party-planning expertise provides the most support and has a variety of contacts for other decor elements. If possible, meet the florist at your ceremony and reception locations. Discuss overall concepts, as well as what atmospheric factors you want the florist to provide and which ones you will take care of. If budget is a consideration, save the bulk of flowers for the reception rather than the ceremony.

Remember, no plan is set in stone. If you want to change the division of labor, or if you need help making decisions, ask the florist for more assistance.

If you prefer to create an individualized floral scheme, round up talented family members and friends who have offered assistance. Walk them through the ceremony and reception spaces and ask for their input on the design and choice of flowers. Look through magazines, wedding photography, and garden and party books for ideas. Collectively come up with

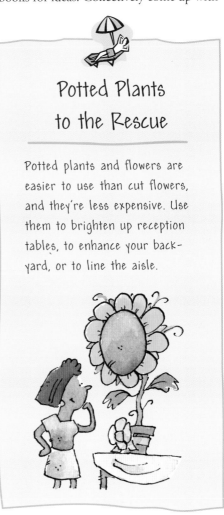

Potted Plants to the Rescue

Potted plants and flowers are easier to use than cut flowers, and they're less expensive. Use them to brighten up reception tables, to enhance your backyard, or to line the aisle.

a scheme and put it down on paper. Then divide up the responsibilities according to the time each person has available and the degree of difficulty. One person can round up the potted plants, another can buy the cut flowers from the produce mart, while someone else may have a beautiful cutting garden and flower-arranging know-how. Put one person in charge of dealing with the florist for complicated arrangements.

USING COLOR

When choosing flowers, you need to take into account what's abundant during the season of your wedding, the particular flowers you've always wanted to carry down the aisle, and the mix of colors that will best enhance your theme.

Potted flowers *transform this birdbath into an unexpected centerpiece. After your wedding, plant the flowers as a romantic reminder.*

The simplest instruction you can give a florist is to emphasize seasonal flowers in a specific color scheme. This is the best way to save money and to ensure an abundance of flowers.

If you've always envisioned a certain flower for the bridal bouquet or you want to get a little more involved in the decision making, there are a number of approaches you can take. For example, you could pick a color scheme and include many different flowers in varying shades of those colors, such as hydrangeas, hyacinths, sweet peas, and forget-me-nots. Or use a single variety of flower that is available in many colors, such as tulips or roses.

A formal wedding can be the easiest of all when it comes to flowers. Simply stick to a monochromatic color scheme, ideally white and ivory. You have an abundance of choices: 'Casa Blanca' lilies, Dendrobium orchids, lilies of the valley, white lilacs, gardenias, peonies, tuberoses, stephanotis, garden roses, and hyacinths. White is also a favorite for less formal occasions; choose casual flowers such as paperwhites, daisies, freesias, and sweet peas. Informal celebrations allow the most flexibility. Select a more vibrant main color such as vivid purple, buttery yellow, or celadon green.

BOUQUETS

It's best to plan your floral scheme around the bridal party before moving on to other areas of the ceremony and reception. Some common spots in the reception site that most typically need flowers are the entrance, the guest tables, the buffet tables (if applicable), and the cake table. You'll probably also want some general floral decor to provide atmosphere. Here's a breakdown of the floral accessories you should think about:

Petals for the flower girl, bouquets for the bride and bridesmaids, boutonnieres for the groom and groomsmen, and corsages are all considered personal flowers.

One of the easiest design concepts for a bouquet is to stick with a single type of flower and one color. If you or a friend is

DECORATING WITH FLOWERS

✳

M AKE THESE DECORATIONS YOURSELF, enlist the help of an artistic friend, or show these photos to your florist. Arrange flowers in your own teapots and vases, borrow vessels from friends, or rent larger containers from a party-supply store. Select seasonal flowers to cut down on cost and to ensure a plentiful supply.

Arrange a cascade of *tiny Dendrobium orchids in a vase or Grecian urn for a formal theme.*

Turn a wrought-iron *candelabra into a rustic welcome sign by twining ivy around the branches. Add half-burned candles, rubbed with gold paint to look old.*

For a simple, *classic nosegay, tie a cluster of similarly colored flowers with a silk ribbon. A friend's beautiful garden roses might do the trick.*

Hang pomanders *of flowers from doorknobs and chandeliers. Let the ribbons trail for a romantic effect.*

Dried Flowers for Diversity

Dried flowers are a simple way to create diversity in your design scheme. Dry them yourself a few months before the wedding, or purchase them at florists, home decor shops, or flower markets. Dried hydrangeas, in particular, make beautiful wreaths—or you can gather them together as an arrangement in a vase.

making the bouquet, tie it by hand with a beautiful satin ribbon in a complementary color for a simple but classic look.

Bridesmaids' bouquets offer a perfect opportunity to show more flower power. Three enticing possibilities are miniature calla lilies, sunny yellow daffodils, and pastel-hued sweet peas, all hard to resist. Although you can keep things easy and wind a simple ribbon around bouquets, wrapping the bouquets in swaths of wispy lace, chiffon, or organza is another beautiful and no-fuss alternative.

Each bridesmaid can carry a bouquet made up of a different hue of the same flower. Or you could put flowers in their hair and have them carry a handkerchief and small Bible as they walk down the aisle during the wedding procession.

The groom's boutonniere should be made to match one of the flowers in the bride's bouquet; boutonnieres and corsages for family members should be influenced

by the bride's bouquet as well. Use the bridesmaids' bouquets as inspiration for the groomsmens' boutonnieres.

As the flower girl walks up the aisle just before the bride's entrance, she can toss petals or a mixture of herbs and flowers to ensure good fortune for the bride. Because the flower girl won't be spreading more than a basketful of petals during her walk, you may want to have a few people blanket the aisle with blossoms just before the ceremony begins. This is a wonderful way to include a few extra friends and relatives in your ceremony. When the flower girl takes her walk, she'll be adding a special touch just for the bride.

OUTDOOR DECORATIONS

When it comes to the ceremony, if your location is a large backyard, an open field, or any other setting that has no obvious focal point, simply highlight the specific spot where you'll be exchanging vows.

Some easy designs that deliver plenty of impact are beautiful urns dripping with asparagus fern, rented blooming fruit trees, a birdbath filled with floating gardenias, vine-covered rented columns, or a trellis. These can easily be purchased or rented at a garden center or through a florist.

INDOOR ADORNMENTS

If your wedding will be held indoors, choose an interior—for example, within a historic building or charming chapel—that does not need any adornment in the first place. If you want to add a floral touch, start by accenting the outside entrance to announce the location of your ceremony. A simple welcoming wreath on the door is perfect. But if you still want to decorate inside, consider the style of the building before you choose your decor. In a stained-glass cathedral, casual terra-cotta pots wouldn't be appropriate for lining the aisle; however, cast-iron torchères draped with vines would be gorgeous.

To trim pews easily, use satin ribbons to hang nosegays of daisies, daffodils, roses, holly, or a bounty of fragrant herbs such as rosemary, thyme, mint, and basil.

Decorating the ceremony aisle or pews is optional. Use flowers if you think they'll really add to the atmosphere. If you have to decorate the aisle, the easiest approach is to line it with some rented low-growing potted trees or plants—olive trees, wispy maidenhair fern—or with rented urns

filled with hydrangeas or paperwhites. To trim pews easily, use satin ribbons to hang nosegays of daisies, daffodils, roses, holly, or a bounty of fragrant herbs such as rosemary, thyme, mint, and basil.

The table at the entrance to the reception serves a double purpose: It provides a warm welcome, and it draws the guests' attention to the guest book and the seating cards you have assembled for them. One cost-effective possibility for adorning this table is to have one of your attendants place her bouquet on the table when she arrives at the reception site.

However, you may decide that you want special floral arrangements for the reception. Here's a good rule of thumb: In a large entrance area, use tall flowers such as a combination of tuberoses, orchids,

Flower marts *are a great place for variety and good prices. Take along a bridesmaid to help you choose, and ask that fresh flowers be held in reserve the morning of the wedding.*

There's no need to overdo the flowers at the ceremony.

'Casa Blanca' lilies, irises, and gladioluses. In a more intimate setting, select shorter flowers such as garden roses, hydrangeas, lilacs, freesias, and tulips.

WHERE TO SPLURGE

Guest tables are the perfect place to splurge on flowers, since your guests will be sitting there the longest. If you're using a florist, look for inspiration in bridal magazine photographs to help you choose the style of centerpiece you'd like best.

of clear glass. Collect the containers from family and friends, or ask your florist to get creative and select a few types.

For informal celebrations, try mixing and matching pots of tulips, daisies, ivy, strawberries, and herbs. Enhance an elegant formal supper-club theme or a classic silver-and-white color scheme by filling silver bowls with lilies of the valley or white peonies, or glass bowls with 'Casa Blanca' lilies or gardenias. For all-around glamour, at each female guest's seat place a single

Guest tables are the perfect place to splurge on flowers. For the simplest approach, arrange garden roses in glass bubble bowls.

For the simplest approach, arrange garden roses in glass bubble bowls (small, spherical containers available from florists). Use flowers that have opened almost fully to achieve the best effect.

To create a sense of quirky individuality, swap the glass bubble bowls for several different types of containers scattered over the guest tables. Try leaf-covered pots, a variety of small urns, or multiple shapes

perfect blossom in a sleek bud vase or float it in a small glass or pottery bowl.

If you've asked your friends to design the arrangements, instruct them either to elevate the flowers high enough or to keep them low enough so that they don't block views and prevent your guests from seeing and conversing with one another.

Tall arrangements work for any degree of formality, depending upon the flowers you choose. The frame usually consists of a towering candelabra or a structure made of wrought iron, silver, glass, wood, or stainless steel that you can rent through floral supply houses or your florist. The flowers and vines are secured at the peak of the frame and wind their way down to the table; a few lie on the surface as if they have fallen.

Accenting the head table or the buffet tables is optional. If you choose to add flowers there, you can do so with a minimum of fuss. Drape premade garlands of greens across the front of each table and pin them into place. Fasten large-headed flowers at all the corners and at the top of each swag—gardenias, hearty roses, and gerbera daisies work well.

Or place a blooming potted rosebush on top of the buffet table. Don't worry if you don't have a planter to place it in; just wrap some fabric or muslin around the base and be done with it. Whimsical topiaries in animal or geometric shapes are also a hit at buffet tables.

Rely on nurseries, your florist, wholesale flower markets, and garden centers to help you find garlands, blooming rosebushes, and topiaries.

FINISHING TOUCHES

At the cake table, the cake is the star, so you don't need to decorate the table with special flowers. If you must have a little extra pizzazz, you can place the bridal and bridesmaids' bouquets on the table. But sometimes the bridal party would rather hold on to them. If that's the case, surround the cake with smilax (a delicate

GIVE ORDINARY CONTAINERS NEW LIFE —REINVENT THEM AS CENTERPIECES FOR TABLES. HERE'S A PAIR OF IDEAS.

Table identifiers

Identify each table for your guests by painting the table number right on the container that holds its floral centerpiece. Or add character by inscribing the container with the names of sentimental songs, addresses like "25 Lover's Lane," or the actual address of your new home.

Draped containers

Cover your bare-bones pots by tying them with fabric. Pale chiffon, warm velvet, crisp linen, and no-fuss muslin all do the trick. Tuck lengths of fabric inside the pot, wrap and tie the ends in an arty knot, and insert the potted flower inside.

EASY BOUTONNIERES

——— ✳ ———

U NSEAT THE TRADITIONAL ROSEBUD BOUTONNIERE and shift to imaginative and beautiful alternatives. To do it yourself, all you need is florist's tape, scissors, a few flowers, and ingenuity. Just think about the flowers you like, then decide if a single bloom or a small spray can be used in your creation.

Accessorize the men *with fragrant sprigs of rosemary. This powerful symbol of remembrance and friendship is bound to bring luck to all who wear it. Add wildflowers for a splash of color.*

Don't underestimate *the effect of a solitary bloom. A single stephanotis pierced with a pearl-headed straight pin is loaded with style.*

Hydrangea florets *offer unexpected detail. Cornflowers, hyacinths, and hibiscus would also work well.*

Holly leaves and berries *win the no-fuss award for holiday weddings. Other great options are pine sprigs, mistletoe, and poinsettia cuttings.*

vine), and pin real or silk flower heads sporadically around a plain tablecloth to create a delightful alternative to store-bought floral tablecloths.

There are additional optional touches that can enhance the atmosphere of the reception and sometimes hide unsightly areas you don't want guests to notice: To mask a clear view of all the kitchen activity when the swinging door opens, or to hide any cumbersome band equipment, rented trees work wonders, turning potential eyesores into ambience.

For an informal wedding held at a home, line the front entrance with blooming potted flowers and then continue the parade indoors and out—atop backyard benches, on windowsills, and along the perimeter of the dance floor. Placing some sprigs of lavender in a bud vase for each bathroom is a nice touch.

ARRANGING YOUR OWN

When putting together your own flower arrangements, set up a miniworkshop with all the right tools close at hand. To give yourself room, set aside a small space in your garage, backyard, or patio.

Get these basic supplies to make the job manageable: buckets to submerge cut flowers in water; sturdy scissors and clippers to trim stems; florist's tape to secure the stems of boutonnieres and corsages; wire frogs (wire forms used in the bottom of containers to hold stems in place); and wet foam brick (also known as floral foam) to anchor flower stems in some center-pieces and larger arrangements. To finish off the bouquets, choose from all the

beautiful ribbons that are available. If you are handling some of the flowers and the florist is arranging the rest, keep in mind that the easiest elements to create are boutonnieres, corsages, bouquets, and baskets of blooms for the flower girl. You should reserve these responsibilities for your own flower-arranging team.

After the wedding celebration has come to a close, you may want to offer your flowers as take-away gifts to special guests or helpers. Or consider donating flower arrangements to a local hospital or nursing home—they'll be appreciated.

SIMPLY PUT...

TERMS OF THE FLORIST TRADE

cascade • A bouquet anchored in a holder with flowers and greens spilling downward like a waterfall.

nosegay • A small, round bouquet of flowers either hand-tied with ribbon or anchored in a bouquet holder.

pomander • A sphere covered with blooms and suspended from a bracelet made of ribbon. A great item for junior bridesmaids or child attendants to wear around their wrists; or you can hang pomanders from doorknobs for dramatic effect.

wired bouquet • Flowers whose stems are supported with wire so they stand upright, then wrapped together to look like one large stem.

AMBIENCE AND DECOR

———— ✳ ————

NO MATTER HOW LITTLE TIME YOU HAVE, YOU CAN CREATE JUST THE SCENE YOU WANT. ALL YOU NEED IS A LITTLE DETERMINATION AND SOME ASTUTE DELEGATING OF RESPONSIBILITIES TO YOUR ATTENDANTS AND WEDDING PLANNER.

Walk through your ceremony and reception areas to see what needs decorative help. List all the spots that need dressing up, and then schedule who will attend to what areas. If you're working with wedding professionals, they'll have a wealth of decorating ideas for you to choose from.

a tent—to flesh out a bare-bones garden site, you're not really helping your budget. Besides, tents are difficult to decorate; you may be better off avoiding them.

The professionals have a few tricks up their sleeves that they pull out for immediate transformations. The good news is

It's often wise to spend more for a fabulous location, because you'll save time and money when it comes to decor.

The easiest way to provide atmosphere is to select a site that has it built in. If you've chosen such a location, you're ahead of the game. It's often wise to spend more for a fabulous location, because you'll save money and time when it comes to decor. If you have to rent costly props—such as

you don't have to be a professional party planner to put them to good use.

Candles are always a popular decorative element and are fairly inexpensive to purchase in quantity. If you're having an evening celebration, you can't beat the glow that a multitude of candles provides.

Enhance the impact of a simple decor element by repeating it on a grand scale.

Put them everywhere—on candelabras lining the aisle, in guests' hands during the ceremony, in the powder rooms, scattered around the garden in paper-bag lanterns, placed upright into the sand at the beach, incorporated into the floral centerpieces, floating in containers.

At an informal affair, use copper or zinc tubs filled with floating candles. A semiformal wedding calls for ceramic or glass candleholders. For formal celebrations, put candles in statuary containers, fountains, pools, or sterling candlesticks.

Your wedding consultant or florist can give you lots of ideas. You can also look through decorating and gardening magazines for inspiration.

LINENS WITH IMPACT

When strategically placed, the right linens transform a room. Your caterer, florist, or site manager can take care of renting tablecloths for you; have them show you what's available. Or rent them yourself from one of the many companies that provide linens at reasonable prices.

If you're marrying at a hotel or resort, you may be offered the banquet linens, but ask to see all the options. There may be a stash of fine linens used in the formal restaurant or reserved for VIP events (of which yours is certainly one). Be assertive so that you can take advantage of the best the location has to offer.

Figure out where linens will have the most impact. Guest tables are a great place to start. For garden weddings, a green-and-white floral pattern is perfect. For a seaside theme, use a plain white cloth covered with

A holiday wedding *is the perfect way to take advantage of seasonal decorations. Trees with lights serve as a magnificent alternative to traditional floral arrangements.*

a pastel blue chiffon overlay. You can never go wrong with a classic damask fabric for formal weddings. White linen hemstitch works in almost any situation regardless of the level of formality.

There's no need for specialty linens on the kids' tables—just use some white butcher paper and make a centerpiece of crayons and colored markers.

GETTING PERSONAL

Since everyone is gathered to celebrate the happy couple, why not accent the space with a few personal items, especially if you're having a home wedding?

A charming touch on the entrance table is a scattering of photos showing the bride and groom from childhood to the present. Put them in frames if there's time.

If you grow your own vegetables and fruits, fill a few decorative bowls with your garden's bounty. Or turn your collection of teapots, vases, or watering cans into receptacles for flowers. Let aspects of your lives show in the decorations. They will add a charming touch to the celebration.

FOCAL POINTS

When scouting locations, keep an eye out for iron gates, pergolas, trellises, sculptures, fountains, or small ponds. If your outdoor location doesn't offer any of these features, consider renting an architectural element to focus attention on the exchange of vows.

It's better to look for a single fantastic piece rather than many props with less impact. Home warehouses, garden centers, iron forgers, florists, and wedding consultants can offer assistance in locating that one strong, show-stopping prop.

As an alternative to renting a focal point, you may wish to create one yourself. Highlight places that need special

Care for Candles

If your candles aren't dripless, be aware of what they might drip on, and move anything out of the way that could get damaged. Put tiles or bases beneath pillar candles to protect furniture surfaces. If children will be attending, keep candles up high and out of reach. Be careful not to place candles anywhere near curtains or dry plants.

attention with decorative accents, flowers, or a combination of both elements. To enhance the area where vows are to be exchanged, use a single prop, such as a trellis, a potted tree, or a statue.

A sand castle is a charming focal point for beach weddings. Enlist bridesmaids, groomsmen, and guests from out of town to build the sculpture during a morning brunch on the beach.

For a home wedding, a mahogany sideboard, decorative screen, or trimmed fireplace mantel does the trick. Garden weddings offer abundant focal points.

HIRING A PRO

If your budget does allow you to hire a professional, use that person to dream up creative ideas, to execute them, or to find the specialty items. Consult with a florist who is also a party designer, or ask your bridal consultant to bring in a designer to help with the overall concept. Either pay such experts just for ideas that you can execute, or ask them to create the full-blown scene. You can add to or subtract from their design as much as you like. Perhaps you can do parts and they can fill in the rest. Some examples:

Go for the cool minimalist look of slipcovered chairs, white china tableware, and uncluttered guest tables with streamlined centerpieces all in classic white or ivory tones. This approach will capture the very essence of simple decor while remaining quite chic.

For a casual reception, offer your guests a truly casual party by hosting an authentic hoedown barbecue. Line the

DECORATIVE ELEMENTS

✴

CREATE A LOOK THAT EXUDES YOUR STYLE AND CREATIVITY. For effortless decor at the reception, scan your shelves for family treasures such as teapots, large bowls, small picture frames, and silver. Use them in unexpected ways to create a fresh attitude.

Dress up the cake *table with a family heirloom. If you don't have a quilt in your family, use a pretty tablecloth or lace bedspread instead.*

For easy ambience, *fill glass bowls with fruit and place them around the house or on the buffet table.*

Personalize *the scene with a variety of framed photographs of the bride and groom. Such a display is perfect for an entrance table at a home wedding.*

Your florist *can create decorative elements like this fruit-studded tree as an alternative to flowers.*

A candelabra hanging *from a tree limb, and an all-white scheme with silver accessories, add elegance to an outdoor reception.*

dance floor with bales of hay and scatter sawdust all around. Hire a Western band, serve a variety of beers instead of fancy cocktails, and set bags of peanuts inside galvanized pails on each table.

Or create an atmosphere that lets your guests get away from it all—without even leaving your reception. You can invent a visual extravaganza featuring elements of another culture. If the couple is going to honeymoon in Mexico, for example, throw a fiesta. Hang piñatas from the ceiling, fill buffet tables with a rainbow of Mexican food, and serve margaritas in hand-blown glassware. Or if one side of the family is Scottish, play up their heritage by hiring bagpipers to wander through the party wearing kilts. Use plaid table linens, and serve a seafood buffet.

SETTING THE MOOD

An evening wedding or reception requires lighting to illuminate the site. You'll also want to consider ambient or decorative lighting—a surefire way to transform an environment. Hang strings of white paper lanterns to create a festive mood. Perhaps skip the floral guest-table centerpieces and use battery-powered lamps highlighted with just a few flowers instead. For day-time weddings, enhance the mood with a wandering mariachi band or string trio, trickling fountains, or burning incense.

You can create ambience in as many ways as there are props and settings. But the best ambience always comes from you and your guests. So even for the most for-mal of weddings, don't overdo the pomp and circumstance. Keep in mind that the main attraction of the day is you and your partner—no matter how much or how little you choose to decorate.

THE MOVABLE FEAST

---*---

YOU DON'T HAVE TO TAKE A CRASH COURSE AT LE CORDON BLEU TO CREATE A SCRUMPTIOUS MENU FOR YOUR WEDDING RECEPTION. YOU JUST HAVE TO KNOW WHAT YOU LIKE. FIND THE STYLE OF CUISINE THAT EXCITES YOU.

Incorporate its flair into your menu and add unique elements of your own to the meal to reflect your tastes.

Start by identifying the type of service appropriate to the style of your wedding. Formal receptions call for a sit-down meal preceded by a cocktail hour including hors d'oeuvres passed around on trays. More relaxed semiformal and informal weddings lend themselves to a single style or a combination of several styles of service: buffet, food stations (main courses that are placed on buffet tables throughout the reception space), seating for the main course only, food passed on trays, family-style, and stationary hors d'oeuvres.

Mix and match the service styles to fit your own needs. The salad course could be served on individual plates by waiters, and the main course served family-style—large platters of the entrée placed at each table. Champagne can be served in the same style, with a few trays being passed and a few platters placed around the room.

WHY USE A CATERER?

A caterer can take care of many elements for you—cuisine, staff, lighting, decor, and entertainment—or provide just some of them. Decide what you need and what you can afford. If you haven't hired any other professional to guide you, let a full-service caterer pick up the slack for you by making recommendations or lining up other pros such as a bartender or even a florist. If you'll be paying the caterer to handle a lot more than the menu, ask for a discount on the total catering package.

A professional caterer will run
the reception according to your schedule.

Explain to the caterer the feeling you're striving for. Do you envision tuxedo-clad waiters serving elegant cuisine, or a casual atmosphere with plenty of dancing and mingling? Talk about what you liked and didn't like at weddings you've attended in the past. Mention any favorite foods you want to include. Then your caterer and you can begin to compose a plan of action, spelling out exactly what will happen.

Let him or her know how long you want the meal service to last. Ask for a packet of food for the busy bride and groom to enjoy later if they don't get an opportunity to eat at the reception.

MEAL PLANS

Next, decide on the specific foods. When you have a choice, incorporate produce that is in season. Seasonal fruits and vegetables are always better tasting and more abundant. Local specialties are also a great place to start. If your celebration brings you seaside, then serving a seafood menu is a breeze. And if a nearby chicken farm promises high-quality fowl, take advantage of its reputation. Seasonal and local foods are almost always lower in price.

The time of year and time of day also play a role. Summer festivities find guests yearning for lighter fare full of fresh fruits and salads. Winter menus call for warmer, more robust dishes (roast chicken instead of chicken salad). For a holiday wedding,

If you love sushi, *feel free to serve it as an hors d'oeuvre. First courses are the best place for unusual foods.*

serve traditional foods and add a few of your favorites. Many dishes can work for either lunch or dinner. Just serve smaller portions for a luncheon. Daytime receptions also require fewer hors d'oeuvres and fewer courses than evening receptions.

If you will be handling the catering responsibilities without a professional, make it easy on yourself. The simplest style of reception is to have an afternoon tea with uncomplicated hors d'oeuvres and finger sandwiches. Since tea is usually served between meals (around 4 P.M.), a full menu is not expected. Much of the food can be made in advance. And lots of dishes served at room temperature will free up valuable space in the refrigerator. It's a good idea to keep the guest count small for this style of reception.

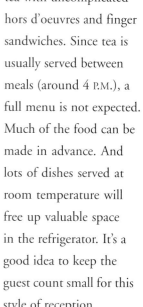

To help streamline your participation, enlist the aid of family and friends. Invite them over to bake cookies, make tea sandwiches, and do the grocery and beverage shopping. Don't attempt to make every dish. Including ready-made items from a take-out establishment is easy and a great way to enhance the menu.

If you want to serve a full-blown meal, remember that restaurants, hotels, and clubs are set up to serve big groups; using one of them would be your simplest solution. Some locations may be problematic because they have small kitchens or none

EASY HORS D'OEUVRES

✳

Y OU WON'T BE IN THE KITCHEN cooking up a storm with these easy appetizers. They're an instant feast for the eyes and the palate. Real food that is easy and elegant does not have to be very fussy or complicated to put together. Pass these ideas on to your caterer, your mom, or your team of volunteers.

Make tiny *Caesar salads by toasting small slices of baguette and piling on the salad. Variations include chopped vegetables or tomato and basil salad.*

Dress up *baby new potatoes with sour cream and a dash of chives. Add a spot of caviar if you feel like splurging.*

Top small polenta *rounds with olive puree or mushroom tapenade. Use rustic ceramic platters to enhance the presentation.*

A versatile *and delicious smoked salmon platter can be placed rather than passed.*

at all, requiring that everything be made beforehand and transported. These are poor choices if you're doing the cooking or you want to serve a hot meal.

To personalize any menu, add something as simple as your grandmother's famous cookies. If you want to include cutting-edge cuisine, incorporate it into the hors d'oeuvres: Guests are more apt to explore new tastes in smaller portions. Experiment with a variety of foods at a tasting well before your wedding day to eliminate any surprises.

HIRING BARTENDERS

Depending on which services your caterer provides, you may need to hire a few more staff members and rent some extra items as well. Your wedding consultant, the site manager, the caterer, and the florist should have suggestions on how to go about staffing up for the reception.

Most weddings need a bartender. Get recommendations from the experts, or call

Some bakeries specialize in wedding cakes; they'll have photos to look through, plus samples. You can also accessorize simple round iced cakes with fresh flowers and piping.

Have One Dessert

Many hotels and restaurants serve a dessert course in addition to the wedding cake. This is overkill. Ask to drop this course. Your guests will flip over your wedding cake, and you'll save money.

a few reputable liquor stores. They're often able to provide bartenders for weddings and other celebrations. You don't need a full bar. Simply hire a bartender to pour wine, beer, and soft drinks.

If you plan to serve mixed drinks and friends have offered to tend bar, purchase a book of drink recipes that they can refer to during the reception, even if they tell you they're experienced.

Whenever possible, supply your own liquor. Many caterers mark up liquor prices tremendously. It's also a smart idea to make some sort of "house" mixed drink —it could be lemonade (regular or with vodka) or a fruit punch (spiked or plain). When prepared in bulk, these beverages are far less expensive than individual mixed drinks that are served by the glass.

Remember, you don't have to host a full bar. Hard liquor, cognac, and liqueurs are the most expensive elements. Instead, you can serve beer, wine, or punch, or set up the bar for a wine tasting with vintages from around the world. Serve champagne for the toast only, making it a special part of the wedding celebration.

OTHER SUPPORT

If you're working with a caterer, confirm that serving staff is included in the package price. If you'll be recruiting the staff yourself, you can still contact local caterers and inquire about hiring a few of their staff for the day. They'll help you figure out how many people you're going to need. Restaurants, cooking schools, and staffing agencies can also send over additional help

You don't need a full bar. Simply hire a bartender to pour wine, beer, and soft drinks.

if necessary. Be specific with the staff about precisely how and when you'd like each course served. Request that everyone dress neatly and appropriately.

A caterer will likely take care of chairs, platters, cutlery, glasses, dishes, and table linens. If not, a local party-rental company can come to the rescue. Most rental companies have a representative who will visit your home or reception site and guide you through the process of renting whatever you'll need. Ask whether they will pick up the equipment afterward and what condition it should be in (for instance, whether all the dishes need to be washed). Review your contracts to determine what your responsibilities are.

Your florist, site manager, or bridal consultant may have quite a few references they would be willing to share with you. Just know that most of the party supplies used by professionals are available at your fingertips—all you have to do is ask.

TIRED OF SERVING THE SAME DRINKS? CHECK OUT THESE FRESH VARIATIONS ON OLD FAVORITES.

Mason-jar margaritas

Ditch the full bar and make waves by serving only classic margaritas and assorted soft drinks in mason jar–inspired mugs.

One for all

Serve one special concoction inspired by your theme—martinis, pitchers of Campari mixed with orange juice, or apéritifs such as Dubonnet with soda and an orange slice.

Iced tea with attitude

Old-fashioned iced tea gets a kick when you stir in strawberries and garnish with mint.

THE PHOTO SHOOT

---✳---

YOUR PHOTO ALBUM TELLS THE STORY OF YOUR WEDDING DAY. IT WILL BE MORE ENGAGING AND TRUE TO LIFE IF YOU INCLUDE SOME NATURAL CANDID SHOTS ALONG WITH THE TRADITIONAL POSED PORTRAITS.

Photographs capture timeless moments, while video captures the energy. Together they document your wedding perfectly, recording the ambience and emotion of events as they unfold throughout the day.

GETTING THE SHOTS

Look for a photographer whose style and sense of humor appeal to you. Word of mouth is the best way to find someone. Perhaps a friend was married recently; was she pleased with the photographer? Or ask your site manager, florist, or even caterer. They may have worked with a fabulous photographer at a previous event, and may have kept his or her card.

Interview a few photographers to see how they differ (see the list on page 131).

When you look at their samples, ask to see an entire wedding shoot, not just the finished album. Sometimes the most telling shots get left out: the flower girl whispering to the bride; the ring bearer asleep on his mother's lap.

If enthusiastic amateurs offer to take photos, accept graciously—but have a pro tackle the main job.

Give the photographer you choose a list of events and the specific pictures you want, including shots of family members and important friends.

Appoint a friend or relative to act as unofficial photographer to help capture

Let your photographer capture the behind-the-scenes glamour.

precious impromptu moments and escort the photographer around. If an enthusiastic amateur offers to take your wedding photos as a gift, accept graciously—but still have a pro tackle the main job.

For a different perspective on your reception, place a disposable camera on each table and attach a note reading, "Please take a photo of everyone at this table, and leave the camera here." Have your attendants encourage guests to use up the whole roll of film.

Traditional belief held that it was bad luck if the bride and groom saw each other right before the ceremony. Today, while we may embrace the gentle innocence of that tradition, we're tempted to break it so we can get the photos out of the way and move on to the fun at the reception. Why not have it both ways?

Have certain photographs taken before you walk down the aisle:

◆ MATRON OF HONOR HELPING THE BRIDE ARRANGE HER VEIL

◆ FATHER PINNING A CORSAGE ON THE BRIDE'S MOTHER

◆ BEST MAN TYING THE GROOM'S BOW TIE

◆ GROOM AND GROOMSMEN IN A STRATEGY HUDDLE

Before the ceremony, have portraits taken of the bride with her attendants and family, and of the groom with his groomsmen and family. Afterward, you can take the remaining wedding-party shots—and still make it to the reception just a few minutes behind your guests.

If you're in the mood for something timeless, ask the photographer to take a few black-and-white shots along with the color ones. Sometimes photographers will use two cameras on site—one for each type of film.

ORDERING PHOTOS

When discussing the specifics with your photographer, see what kind of wedding photo packages are available. You can order an album, an album with reprints, or just reprints. Packages tend to vary widely from one photographer to another, but overall it's usually much less expensive to order a predetermined number of reprints and the album as a complete set.

You may want to include photos with your thank-you cards or give both sets of parents albums they can keep for themselves. Some photographers will charge a fee for film processing in addition to the fee for the album package, depending on the package you decide to order.

SIMPLY PUT...

PHOTOGRAPHIC TERMS

proofs • Small sample photographs that show what shots the photographer took. These are used as a guide in ordering albums, enlargements, and duplicate photos for friends and family.

styling • The arranging of people, objects, and wardrobe in a photo. When the photographer fluffs the veil and moves the ring bearer closer to the flower girl, that's known as styling.

Your photographer will send proofs to you shortly after the wedding. (If you're using a magnifying glass to examine the proofs, don't be alarmed by the pimple on your cheek—most photographers will do a bit of retouching for an additional fee.) You'll have the finished pictures within a few weeks to a couple of months.

A VIDEO TO REMEMBER

Perhaps you'd like a video camera to catch the action of your wedding from beginning to end. Why not? A video is a terrific way to record the event and capture the enjoyment of your guests while conveying all the emotion and drama of the big day.

There are two schools of thought concerning video style, and both techniques work well to capture the magic of your wedding day. The first approach is the one-camera, or documentary-style, video. The videographer simply shoots the event from beginning to end using one camera, with little editing in mind. The cost is relatively low. The two-camera, or highlight, video is the second approach. With two cameras,

A Private Screening

To unwind in your new home after the wedding hubbub, make a date with each other for dinner and a movie. Make dinner a candlelight affair for two. The movie? Your wedding video, sure to receive rave reviews!

the videographer has a couple of angles to edit from to create one seamless video that highlights the best parts of your wedding and reception. Naturally, this two-camera technique will cost a bit more.

The best way to find a good videographer is by word of mouth. To guarantee success, make sure you're hiring a professional.

Using a combination of the two is also an option. Instead of paying for two cameras, include a friend who offers to videotape your wedding as a gift. Ask the videographer to shoot the wedding as he sees it and use the footage from your friend's video as additional material for editing. Introduce them prior to the wedding so your friend is aware that the two of them will be collaborating.

If you choose to use only one camera, don't assign that job to a friend. If there are technical problems and the tape is ruined, or if you don't like what you see, it may compromise your friendship. This is a case in which you're certainly better off with a professional.

FINDING A PRO

The best way to find a videographer is by word of mouth. To guarantee success, make sure you're hiring a professional. Start with your photographer. Some studios also provide video service and can include it as part of your photo package.

If not, ask other wedding vendors, family, and especially people who have been married recently. When interviewing a videographer, review entire videos from several actual weddings instead of looking only at the videographer's demo reel, which presents only highlights of the videographer's best work. If one of the sample videos captures the feeling you want for your wedding video, you know you have found someone you can work with. Here are some key elements you should look for:

◆ SMOOTHLY FLOWING EDITS

◆ GOOD AUDIO QUALITY

◆ COMPREHENSIVE SCOPE, CAPTURING ALL THE ACTION

If the videographer's brochure is full of technical jargon, don't be shy about pressing for clarification. The process is simple, so you shouldn't let these complicated terms deter you from asking questions when you don't understand something completely (see the list on page 132).

CAPTURING AUDIO

The easiest and most discreet way to capture the audio from the ceremony is to outfit the officiant with a cordless microphone (the videographer will supply one). It will pick up the officiant's words as well as the exchanging of the vows. Lightweight and unobtrusive, these microphones are small technical wonders.

Decide what kind of audio from the reception is important, such as toasts and special vocalists or comments from well-wishing guests. Videographers will usually record music over all other audio.

If bright lights and staged interviews are not what you'd like to record for posterity, let the videographer know that you

A journalistic approach *to the photography documents precious, private moments with loved ones on your wedding day.*

would prefer to have candid moments and ambient atmosphere recorded using the lighting that's available.

Avoid misunderstandings by giving the videographer a schedule of events. That way the videographer can plan ahead and time coffee breaks. You want to be sure the camera is right there "rolling" when you're cutting the wedding cake.

The videographer can probably supply you with as many copies of the finished tape as you would like. You might want to compare these prices with those of a video-duplicating service bureau.

Instead of paying extra for multiple titles and graphics within the video, the best addition to the live footage is incorporating a photographic montage. Supply the photographs to your videographer and ask that they be included. This is a wonderful way to end the video.

COUNTDOWN to the
Big Day

—✳—

1 Drink 8 to 10 glasses of water daily so that your skin will be **clear and glowing** on your wedding day. **2** Condition your hair regularly and **deep-condition** in the months leading up to the wedding. **3** **Reduce stress** by meeting with your officiant beforehand to review the ceremony step-by-step. **4** Invite everyone involved in the **ceremony** to the rehearsal. Go over the procession and recession several times. **5** Keep the **rehearsal dinner** small and manageable by inviting just parents and the wedding party. **6** For great atmosphere, ask that the **bells** at your place of worship be rung after the pronouncement. **7** Pick the **music** you like best for the ceremony, whether it's rock and roll or Broadway show tunes. **8** Include music that has a significant meaning, such as the **song** that was playing the first time you kissed. **9** Personalize the ceremony by writing a portion of your vows or including a **family tradition.** **10** Ask the best man to arrange for guest **transportation** to the reception. ●

GOIN' TO THE
CHAPEL

PREPARING FOR THE CEREMONY

* —— * —— *

The trick to creating a unique wedding is to blend time-honored customs with new traditions you choose yourselves. It needn't be complicated. Simply add a few personal touches: your favorite music, readings by friends or family members, a vocal performance, or original vows.

Get together with the wedding party for a thorough rehearsal. Be sure that everyone knows what his or her duties are for the big day. Celebrate afterward with a simple dinner. Don't worry whether the festivities will come off without a hitch. Those impromptu glitches are what add character and spontaneity to any wedding.

To look and feel your best, start focusing on healthful habits now. Taking care of yourself will pay off when you walk down the aisle looking wonderful. Plan your hair and makeup well in advance and practice both ahead of time so you can be confident and relaxed on your wedding day.

LOOKING YOUR BEST

---✳---

NATURALLY, THE TWO OF YOU WANT TO PUT YOUR BEST FOOT FORWARD FOR YOUR WEDDING DAY—AND ALSO FOR POSTERITY, CONSIDERING ALL THE PHOTOS YOU'LL BE IN. IT'S NOT TOO EARLY TO START PAMPERING YOURSELVES.

Although it probably sounds like a cliché, a radiant appearance starts on the inside. If you take care of yourself physically and emotionally, you'll project that glowing aura of happiness when the big day arrives. (That's not to say that you can't give the outer you a little help, however.)

The keys to success are simple: Eat healthful foods, exercise regularly, and get plenty of rest. Not only will you reduce your stress and boost your energy, but you'll be slimmer and more toned. Forget about starving yourself or training like an Olympic athlete. Just cut back on fatty, processed foods; eat more fruits and vegetables; and do 30 minutes of aerobic exercise three times per week.

The exercise needn't be strenuous, nor need it involve a complex regimen. Taking walks with your fiancé while you discuss wedding plans will work wonders for your physique. Or enroll at a nearby gym for aerobics, dance, or yoga classes.

If you keep the main objective in mind —looking and feeling fabulous—exercise will be a pleasure rather than another task. In fact, if you make exercise a habit now, you and your fiancé just might stick with your routine after the wedding day is over.

When it comes to hair and makeup, don't try to change your look dramatically for the big day. Simply concentrate on enhancing your best features and let your happiness shine through.

SKIN-CARE TIPS

For glowing skin, drink 8 to 10 glasses of water per day before the wedding. Water naturally cleanses your body of impurities. If you're not accustomed to drinking that much, work up to it gradually. Avoid alcohol as much as possible because it dries out

Dealing With Pimples

If a blemish pops up on your face the morning of your wedding day, don't panic and don't pick, push, or squeeze. Instead, take the red out with eyedrops. Place a few drops on a cotton ball and hold it on the pimple for about 15 seconds.

your skin (with all those engagement parties, this one takes discipline). Also avoid the foods that cause breakouts for you.

Next, assess your current skin-care regimen. If your complexion looks great, don't change a thing. But if it could use a little help, consult a dermatologist, beauty consultant, or makeup artist for tips.

The standard components of a basic skin-care regimen consist of three simple steps: cleansing, toning, and moisturizing. Exfoliating your skin and applying masks help remove dead cells. Shop around for skin-care products; you can always try out samples from department store counters or beauty salons until you find the right line for you. But be sure you start early: you don't want to find that you're allergic to a new moisturizer the night before the wedding. For an extra dose of pampering, many brides—and even some grooms—treat themselves to a salon facial a week or so before the wedding day.

HELP FOR HAIR

Dry, brittle hair can be a vexing problem, but it's easy to fix in time for the wedding. Just be sure to use a good conditioner regularly, and deep-condition each weekend for 10 to 30 minutes. Also, try at least one hot-oil treatment in a beauty salon or at home a few weeks before the big day.

Have your hair trimmed regularly—every six weeks for long hair, as needed for shorter styles. Ideally, the groom should get a haircut about two weeks before the wedding to avoid that just-shorn look.

If either of you is considering a radically new style, try it out several months

If you're wearing a veil, *you'll look picture-perfect on the big day by choosing a hairstyle that works with the veil's fit and design.*

ahead of time to prevent last-minute disasters. Brides will do best if they adhere to classic hairstyles such as a chignon, French twist, ponytail, or bob. Wearing your hair up or pulled back adds an instant touch of elegance, shows off your face, and is much easier to manage (no combing or last-minute adjusting is required).

You know what makes you the most comfortable, so don't be talked into something that's not right for you. Whether you'll be doing your own hair or using a professional stylist, practice the look with your veil or headpiece beforehand, and allow yourself an hour for styling your hair on the wedding day.

If you do your own haircoloring, limit yourself to subtle changes and use a product that has automatic shutoff ingredients so you won't damage your hair. Hand over drastic changes or highlights to the pros.

The blushing bride *can stay that way—with a little help. Dust powder over your face and lips to keep cosmetics in place.*

Again, don't try an experiment too close to the big day. Hair that's colored or highlighted regularly should be touched up about two weeks prior to the wedding.

MAKEUP MAGIC

This is no time to experiment with new looks. The best approach is also the simplest: Stick with your usual color palette but apply makeup a little more heavily.

If you're doing your own makeup, just apply it as you normally would for dressy occasions. Allow yourself plenty of time (at least one hour) to do your best work, and use a well-lit mirror. The essentials are foundation, neutral eye shadow, soft eyeliner, concealer, blush, waterproof mascara, neutral lipstick and liner, and powder.

A simple way to keep your makeup fresh throughout the festivities is to apply your cosmetics, then dust powder on your face and lips. Apply lipstick over powder for glossier-looking lips.

Plan to adjust your makeup for the special demands of photography. Color film intensifies whatever is already bold,

so avoid frosted makeup and use neutral tones for face, eyes, and lips. Black-and-white film whitens pale colors and darkens strong colors, so avoid red lipstick (it will look black) and blend away any harsh lines if you will be posing for black-and-white photos. Be sure to wear a light moisturizer under your foundation. Heavy creams will show through makeup quickly and give your face a shiny appearance.

Want a pro to apply your makeup? It's a cinch. Ask for referrals from friends and relatives, a beauty salon, or a department store's cosmetic counter. Try out a few different professionals, and take a photograph after each application to see how it looks in photos. Write down the colors each artist uses in case either one of you forgets.

The best approach is also the simplest: Stick with your usual color palette but apply your makeup a little more heavily.

Relaxing will also help you look your best. On the day before the wedding, indulge in a yoga session, meditation, a massage, or a long, hot bath with scented candles— they all promote deep relaxation. To help with prewedding jitters, the groom can try meditation and a massage, or treat himself to a professional shave at a barbershop, complete with hot towels.

Play tapes of your favorite music and enjoy some healthful snacks while you do your hair and makeup. If you find yourself getting nervous, remember that the two of you are not giving a performance. All you have to do is be yourselves.

CEREMONY LOGISTICS

———— ✳ ————

Y OU AND YOUR PARTNER HAVE QUITE A LOT OF LEEWAY WHEN IT COMES TO ORCHESTRATING YOUR PROCESSION AND RECESSION. EVEN IN A RELIGIOUS CEREMONY, YOU CAN USUALLY ADAPT THE SERVICE TO YOUR PREFERENCES.

The first step is to meet with your officiant to review the ceremony in detail. For simplicity, stick with the basic outline your officiant recommends and make only small variations. If you have your heart set on a more customized ceremony, realize that such changes could require more time and effort on the part of all concerned.

The ceremony outline that follows is a traditional one for a Christian wedding, whether it is held in a garden or a church. Your officiant will be able to advise you on changes that your particular denomination finds acceptable.

Once the details of your ceremony have been decided upon, ask for a written outline from your officiant or wedding planner so you can review each element of the service and plan accordingly.

Planning your ceremony will be easier if you understand all the individual parts. Here's a quick breakdown.

The *prelude* refers to the half hour or so prior to the wedding ceremony when guests are taking their seats.

For the *procession,* which signals the beginning of the ceremony, the wedding party parades down the aisle to the altar. The officiant greets everyone and makes opening remarks during the *welcome.*

In the *charge,* the officiant confirms that the bride and groom are marrying of

Schedule a rehearsal beforehand and go through it several times so each participant knows what to do.

his and her own free will. Next comes the *exchange of vows,* as the bride and groom make promises to each other; then the *exchange of rings,* during which the bride and groom offer rings to each other as symbols of their never-ending love.

During the *pronouncement,* the officiant announces that the bride and groom are husband and wife (this is the "kiss the bride" part). Finally, the *recession* marks the ceremony's close. The wedding party exits up the aisle, followed by the guests.

ORDER, ORDER!

Decide on the order of the bridal party for the procession and recession. Many places of worship don't specify just how it should go, so here's a guideline that works for all types of ceremonies.

The officiant walks down the aisle at the head of the procession, followed by the groom and his parents, then the best man. If the groom's parents won't be accompanying him, the best man can walk down the aisle alongside the groom. Next come the groomsmen and bridesmaids

> **For an easy touch of atmosphere, ask that the bells at your place of worship be rung after the pronouncement.**

(together or separately), followed by the honor attendant. The ring bearer and the flower girl are next. (They can arrive together; if they walk separately, the flower girl follows the ring bearer.) The last one down the aisle is the bride, accompanied by her father, mother and father, or escort.

For the recession, first up the aisle is the happy couple, followed by the ring

---

CEREMONY SEATING

ARE YOU TRYING TO FIGURE OUT WHERE each of your guests will sit during the wedding ceremony? Relax. You can make the seating arrangement as simple as you choose. Pick any one of the following uncomplicated—yet traditional—plans.

Simple
Enclose small seating cards in invitations sent to family members and other special guests. These guests simply hand the cards to the ushers, who escort them to seats marked "reserved."

Simpler
Ask the ushers to seat the bride's family on the left (as you face the pulpit) and the groom's family on the right. Reserve the front row for parents and the second row for grandparents and siblings.

Simplest
Seat guests all together. Mark the front few rows as reserved for family. Have your ushers ask if guests are family members so the ushers will know where to seat them.

Let Others Run the Rehearsal

Put the rehearsal on cruise control by letting the officiant or wedding coordinator run the show. Go over the details and let your thoughts be known prior to the rehearsal. Then sit back and enjoy the ride. Steer clear of confusion by avoiding major changes in the script at this point. Unless you need to make a vital adjustment, simply leave things as they are.

bearer and flower girl, side by side. Next come the honor attendant and best man together, followed by the bridesmaids and groomsmen in pairs (if the wedding party is an odd number, one groomsman can walk with two bridesmaids, or a groomsman can walk alone). The parents of the bride are followed by the groom's parents. These guidelines are flexible, so feel free to adapt them however you like.

For an easy touch of atmosphere, ask that bells at your place of worship be rung after the pronouncement as you start the recession. If you are marrying outside a place of worship, ask your entertainment provider to include an uplifting recording of bells as the two of you kiss or as you walk up the aisle as husband and wife.

REHEARSAL STRATEGIES

Nothing will de-stress your wedding as effectively as a good rehearsal. Hold it a

day or two before the ceremony and invite the entire bridal party, plus anyone else who has special duties during the wedding. Ask the photographer and videographer to stop by; it will be helpful for them to see the sequence of events. And it's always a good idea to round up a few of the musicians to play during the rehearsal. If that's not possible, ask that at least one of the musicians attend the rehearsal and bring a tape or a CD. Hearing the music will help everyone with the correct timing.

As for planning the rehearsal, you can delegate the task to your wedding planner or to a member of your wedding party.

It's not necessary to go through the entire ceremony at the rehearsal; just practice any parts that include a special cue or other elements that a member of the bridal party needs to watch for. Practice where

Traditionally, the bride stands *to the groom's left, with the best man and the honor attendant flanking the couple.*

everyone will stand upon reaching the altar. This gives each participant a specific place to head to when walking down the aisle. Then run through the entire procession and recession several times.

Traditionally, the bride stands to the left of the groom at the head of the aisle. On the bride's left stands her honor attendant, and on the groom's right side is his

bridesmaids standing shoulder to shoulder in a straight or diagonal line just behind the bride and the honor attendant, and the groomsmen similarly lined up just behind the groom and his best man.

The bride's parents sit on the aisle, in the front row, left. The groom's parents sit on the aisle, in the front row, right. If any children will be included in the ceremony,

In years past, the groom's family always hosted the rehearsal dinner, but today anyone can take it on—or you can elect not to have one.

best man. When the bride has two honor attendants, they should stand shoulder to shoulder to the left of the bride.

The bridesmaids and groomsmen can either form a semicircle around the bride and groom or stand separately, with the

Rehearsal Dinner Fun

Ask guests to bring to the rehearsal dinner their favorite framed photograph of themselves with the bride or groom. Place a photo or two on each table or arrange them on one table near the entrance to the party. These are great conversation pieces and might include a range of photos from childhood to the present. Make sure the photos are returned to the guests at the end of the party.

the flower girl can stand in front of the bridesmaids or sit with her parents. Similarly, the ring bearer can stand in front of the groomsmen. He could also give the rings to the best man and honor attendant, and then sit with his parents.

If you feel a bit nervous about giving the ring bearer responsibility for the wedding bands, just tie fake rings to the ring pillow, then have the best man and honor attendant hold the real ones.

The best man holds the bride's ring for the groom, and the honor attendant holds the groom's ring for the bride.

THE ROLE OF USHERS

At most weddings, the groomsmen act as the ushers. Brief them on the best way to show guests to their seats. There are two easy ways to seat guests. For formal ceremonies, the usher offers his right arm to a female guest; her escort follows behind. While they walk, the usher explains the seating pattern (bride's side, groom's side, or mixed together). For less formal occasions, the usher can simply show guests to

Avoid stress by having the wedding party arrive well in advance, dressed and ready for the ceremony.

their seats without offering his arm to the ladies. However formal you decide to be, the usher should offer to escort the eldest woman to her seat first when many guests arrive at the same time.

Have your ushers arrive an hour early and then gather near the guests' entrance about a half hour prior to the ceremony.

THE REHEARSAL DINNER

It's traditional to top off the rehearsal with a dinner party. In years past, the groom's family always hosted the rehearsal dinner, but today anyone can take it on. You can also elect not to have the dinner—it's by no means a requirement.

If the responsibility for the rehearsal dinner falls to you, there are ways to make sure it stays simple. Keep the invitation

list small. Invite both sets of parents; the wedding party, along with their spouses or dates; and the parents of child attendants. If you want a larger crowd, include grandparents and out-of-town guests.

Have the meal at a restaurant or club. Offer cocktails at your place (or that of a family member) first if you're operating on a tight budget. Often the liquor is the most expensive part of a dinner. Another alternative to preparing a meal is to have it catered at someone else's home. If that's not an option, opt for a barbecue, brunch, or buffet—they're all easier and less stressful than organizing a sit-down dinner.

Ideally, schedule the rehearsal and the dinner for a day or two before the ceremony, so that everyone has plenty of time to rest up before the wedding.

MAKING IT PERSONAL

---　✳　---

B Y ITS VERY NATURE, EACH MARRIAGE IS UNIQUE. IN JOINING TOGETHER, THE TWO OF YOU COMBINE YOUR OWN SPECIAL HISTORIES. WITH A LITTLE INGENUITY AND WITH LITTLE FUSS, YOU CAN PERSONALIZE YOUR CEREMONY, TOO.

Wedding ceremonies are sometimes so traditional that you forget there are simple things you can do to make your wedding unique. Consider one of the following:

Have the groom meet the bride in the aisle. The bride and her escort walk about three-quarters of the way down the aisle, where the groom is waiting for her. The escort gives the bride to the groom. The bride and groom walk down the rest of the aisle together. This allows guests sitting farther back to feel closer to the ceremony, and the bride and groom to feel more united as they approach the officiant.

Switch places with your officiant. Stand side by side facing your guests; they will enjoy seeing you recite your vows.

Write a portion of your vows. Incorporate a few of your thoughts on trust, friendship, faith, respect, forgiveness, or honor into the vows that your officiant

However you involve your family, it's a simple way to make them feel special and help the celebration reflect your values.

provides you with. Keep your thoughts short and sweet. Write them down and, if you can, carry them with you in case nervousness causes you to forget.

Include readings. Invite a close family member or friend to read a special poem or tell a brief anecdote about your courtship or how you met. This is especially effective if presented by the person who introduced you. Ask to see a copy of the reading first, however, to be sure it's not embarrassing.

Involve your parents. Ask both sets of parents to greet your guests at the entrance to the ceremony, to make a welcome statement, or to accompany both the bride and groom during the procession.

Include more family and friends. This is a favorite way to personalize your big day.

SIMPLY PUT...

CEREMONIES

civil • Usually a short ceremony with no religious affiliation. Can be performed by a judge.

religious • Performed by a clergy member of a particular faith.

interfaith • When the couple are members of different religions. They can combine the two services to include elements of each, or they can turn to a clergy member from one religion who is willing to marry them.

If you have children from a previous marriage, make them part of the ceremony. Ask the officiant to bless pendants, which may then be given to children at the same time the bride and groom exchange rings.

Ask aunts, uncles, cousins, or grandparents to start the wedding by leading off the procession with a candle-lighting ceremony. Have ushers pass out candles to guests as they are seated; then, as your family members walk down the aisle, they stop at each row and light a guest's candle. Or ask a few of the older children or teenagers to light the candles at the altar during the ceremony. You can also include all the children in your family, dressed up in fine suits and pretty dresses, by asking them to line the path as the procession makes its way down the aisle.

However you involve your family, it's a simple way to make them feel special and help the celebration reflect your values.

Work in cultural traditions. It's easy to include one or more traditional elements

A huppa, or prayer-cloth canopy, is a religious symbol used in Jewish weddings. Here, swaths of filmy fabric have been tied to poles with bouquets of flowers.

as an acknowledgment of your heritage. Just ask grandparents or parents for ideas. Here are a few common customs: Jewish couples break a glass as a reminder that life is bittersweet. In China, the bride and groom drink cups of wine tied together with string to symbolize their new bond. At English weddings, the wedding party walks together to the ceremony to symbolize unity. African-American couples jump over a broom to signify a break from their pasts. In Spain, the groom gives the bride 13 coins to show his ability to support her.

Greet each guest. Form a receiving line at the reception. If time and space allow, a receiving line gives the bride, groom, and parents an opportunity to have a personal moment with every guest.

Add religious symbols. Turn to your religions to personalize your ceremony.

If you are Catholic, ask your priest about performing a nuptial mass, and include some of your favorite scriptures, prayers, and hymns. This celebration is usually held at noon, which is perfect for an afternoon luncheon reception.

If you are Jewish, surround yourself with a prayer-cloth canopy, traditionally called a *huppa*. Many florists rent *huppas* then decorate them with flowers and vines. The support posts can be made out of anything from rustic tree branches to wrought iron with intricate finials. Ask young children to hand out yarmulkes to male guests as they enter the ceremony area.

If you want a particular scripture to personalize your ceremony but you don't remember where it is in the Bible, you may be able to locate it in a religious concordance book, which you can find at libraries or bookstores. Key words are listed in alphabetical order, with the location of the verse or phrase listed next to them.

Small gestures make a wedding memorable. Pass out special prayers, poems, or readings for your guests to recite together. For a small gathering, ask the officiant to invite guests to surround you at the altar as you exchange vows. Honor a deceased parent, relative, or friend with a special mention during the ceremony. As a playful touch for an out-of-doors wedding, include your dogs as "flower dogs" and have them walk down the aisle with children or sit near the front row.

FAVORITE MUSIC

Music is another simple way to fill the ceremony with warmth. Contemporary rock, Broadway show tunes, and jazz—with lyrics or as instrumentals—are all acceptable styles. Include songs that have significant meaning to you: for example, the tune that was playing when you first kissed or when one of you proposed.

Decide whether you want the music to be recorded or performed live. Perhaps you want a combination of the two. Ask your site manager or someone at your place of worship if there are any restrictions regarding music and whether a sound system is available for you to use.

If you're getting married in a place of worship, it's easiest to use affiliated musicians—the soloist, organist, or choir.

If you don't have a musician in mind, ask around. Word of mouth is, as always, the best recommendation. Check with your place of worship, the manager of the

Call on Talented Friends

Instead of hiring a vocalist, ask talented friends or relatives to sing just before the procession begins or just after you exchange vows. (Be sure you have heard them sing prior to asking them to perform!) Help choose the piece, and invite them to participate in the rehearsal—it's a simple way to make your wedding ceremony more personal.

Have a singer perform your favorite music, even if it's show tunes.

reception location, the musicians' union, party rental places, your bridal consultant, and, of course, family members, friends, and acquaintances who are music fans.

To keep things really simple, hire just one musician—a pianist, an organist, or a harpist for the ceremony. To include a few more, have a trio (violin, flute, and harp), a string quartet (two violins, viola, and cello), or a brass ensemble (French horn, trumpets, trombone, and a baritone sax).

To figure out what your musical needs are, determine which phases of the ceremony require accompaniment. Traditionally, music is played during the:

◆ HALF-HOUR PRELUDE, WHEN GUESTS TAKE THEIR SEATS
◆ PROCESSION
◆ BRIDE'S WALK DOWN THE AISLE
◆ RECESSION (CHOOSE AN UPLIFTING PIECE OF MUSIC)

Quiet chamber music offers a meditative backdrop while guests take their seats. If

you want a dramatic entrance, have the church choir sing as the wedding party makes its way down the aisle. Consider using a nontraditional symphony piece for the bride's walk. And for a dramatic recession with little effort, hire trumpeters to line the aisle and play a jubilant tune.

Double-Duty Musicians

Simplify the music planning by using the same performers for both the ceremony and reception. Check with the band and music departments of your local colleges or universities. Many students are talented and eager for experience and extra cash. Post a notice giving particulars, and responses will roll in.

TRANSPORTATION IDEAS

---✳---

HOW TO GET THE WEDDING PARTY AND OUT-OF-TOWN GUESTS TO THE CEREMONY AND FROM THERE TO THE RECEPTION? THE EASY ANSWER IS TO LET GUESTS AND ATTENDANTS TAKE CARE OF THEIR OWN TRANSPORTATION.

But if you feel that your guests will need some help, make a list of the transportation requirements and ask the best man or another member of the wedding party to pitch in with the arrangements. (It's the best man's responsibility to get the groom to the ceremony; afterward, the bride and groom travel together.)

Minivans are a lower-cost alternative to limousines with drivers. Arrange to rent them through a car leasing company, and ask friends and family members to act as chauffeurs for your guests.

The ceremony may be over, *but you're still in the limelight. After a private moment, emerge and let attendants shower you.*

There are loads of options for arriving in style at either location. It's a good idea to see the vehicle or other mode of transportation in person and to interview potential drivers before you make a final decision.

If the ceremony and reception are in different locations, enjoy a private toast on the way. You may not be alone together for a while!

A caravan of limousines is always a good way to go. Your local fire or police stations may have antique fire engines or paddy wagons for rent. How about a double-decker bus or trolley car? Consider hiring a horse-drawn sleigh if it will be a winter wedding and you can count on snow. If you're marrying near a lake or pier, a boat allows the bride and her escort to make a splashy entrance. If you want to be adventurous, arrive on a motorcycle and in a sidecar—it's a sure way to get attention.

Be sure to provide drivers with directions to all the locations where they'll be picking up and dropping off the couple or the guests. (This is another task that can be delegated to the best man.) Request that all drivers be well groomed, dressed according to your requirements (tuxedo, uniform, or theme costume), courteous, and prepared with large umbrellas in case of rain. To avoid any potential mix-ups, get rental details in writing before putting down your deposit, and reconfirm all the plans about a week before the wedding.

Once you've made the arrangements, perhaps your wedding party will surprise you with a special touch. The traditions of tying old shoes or tin cans to the back of the newlyweds' vehicle originally were thought to ward off evil spirits. Less noisy alternatives: a posy of flowers tied to the side-view or rearview mirrors, satin ribbon on the door handles, or a "Just Splendidly Married" sign in the window.

A PRIVATE MOMENT

If the ceremony and reception are held at the same location, plan a special moment for yourselves after you say your "I do's." Whether you retreat to your hotel suite or to some other private spot, a few quiet moments together will help you appear relaxed and at ease for the reception.

As your guests find their way to the reception, ask your wedding coordinator, caterer, or site manager to set aside a bottle of champagne and hors d'oeuvres for you to enjoy alone. This is a time when you can make your own personal toasts, reflect on the excitement of the ceremony, and reminisce about what you thought when you first glimpsed one another.

If the ceremony and reception are at different locations, enjoy a private toast on the way to the reception. Chances are you won't have another private moment until the end of the reception, so take the scenic route if you have time.

LEAVE THE CEREMONY OR RECEPTION IN A SHOWER OF GOOD LUCK. ATTENDANTS CAN ARRANGE ONE OF THESE TOKENS.

Perfect potpourri

Many stationers sell these potpourri-filled cones, but it's easy to make your own. Roll a paper doily, or paper ingrained with dried flowers, into a cone. Pour in dried potpourri. Seal the edges with a foil sticker.

Friendly birdseed

Birdseed is kinder than rice to the birds who feast on it after your departure. Pour it into small muslin bags, and ask an eager child or family member to pass them out.

Tiny bubbles

This is a whimsical touch that guests can employ after the ceremony or during the reception. As the two of you are dancing your first dance, guests surround the dance floor and envelop you with bubbles.

STRATEGIES to
MAKE it Easy

—✳—

1 To **simplify** your day, eliminate optional parts of the reception that don't appeal to you. **2** Make a special entrance as a couple. After everyone is seated, walk **hand in hand** to the dance floor for the first dance. **3** Make sure there's a **drop-off point** in the parking lot for elderly or disabled guests. **4** Ask the best man to contact family and friends who may want to **give speeches.** He can help them prepare their toasts. **5** Give each vendor and member of the wedding party a **schedule** detailing the timing for all events. **6** Ask your stationer for a few blank place cards, in case any **unexpected** guests show up. **7** Give **party favors** as elegant as silver picture frames or as casual as tiny wicker baskets filled with candy. **8** Figure out **tips** ahead of time and give the host or wedding coordinator envelopes to distribute. **9** Mix fresh faces with **longtime acquaintances** in the seating plan. ●

PLANNING
YOUR RECEPTION

YES, YOU CAN RELAX AND ENJOY IT

*　　※　　*

Gone are the days when bride and groom were banished to the end of a receiving line to greet guests in morning coats and scratchy crinolines. These days, a wedding reception is a party—and when it's your wedding, you call the shots. So choose what you'd like most to do and what makes planning simplest. You and your guests can dance on a rooftop with a glittering city as your backdrop, romp on a sandy beach, or dine by candlelight in a country garden. Make your choice easy, memorable, and fun for guests—and especially for you.

Even the most lighthearted reception takes careful planning. Here's the secret: The more carefully you plan, the more you can relax and enjoy the big day. Break down the details into small, manageable tasks. Friends and relatives may take pleasure in giving you their ideas and pitching in. Along with the professionals, they can share the load so that you'll have time to enjoy yourself at the reception.

CREATING A SCHEDULE

---✳---

T HE WELL-PLANNED RECEPTION UNFOLDS IN A SERIES OF LOVELY EVENTS. KEEPING THEM SIMPLE AND WORKING OUT THEIR SEQUENCE WILL HELP THE DAY FLOW MORE SMOOTHLY AND ENSURE THAT YOU WON'T FEEL RUSHED.

Begin by jotting down some of the highlights of the reception in the order of their occurrence (the arrival of guests, cocktail hour, the beginning of the meal, and so on). Then start filling in the fine points (the first dance, toasts, cake cutting, the bouquet and garter toss).

Once you're ready to devise a schedule, refer to the sample on the next page to get an idea of the elements involved and the generally accepted timing for each. To set your mind at ease, put your wedding consultant or a volunteer in charge of monitoring the flow of the party; that person should remind you when it's time to move on to the next event. After all, you don't want the musicians to be packing up their instruments before you cut the cake!

What elements would you like to include in your reception? Consider each of the following traditions; feel free to add to or subtract from the list, or to include your own personal choices.

The receiving line. This custom is purely optional. At a large affair, the receiving line gives everyone a chance to greet the bride, groom, and parents. For a simpler wedding, it's easy to forgo. Decide whether you'd rather greet each guest one by one on the line, or wander from table to table throughout the reception.

For simplicity's sake, it's a good idea to form the receiving line at the ceremony location, right after the wedding ends. That makes your guests' path clear: They can proceed through the line, greet you

Plan a simple sequence of events to
avoid feeling rushed.

RECEPTION TIMETABLE

✳

MOST RECEPTIONS LAST FROM THREE TO FIVE HOURS and begin no more than a half hour after the ceremony. To help simplify your planning, use this outline for a four-hour reception that includes dinner. Adjust it to fit the length of your reception, and whether the occasion is a dinner, cocktail reception, luncheon, or tea.

Morning. The party-rental company arrives at the site to set up tables and chairs and drop off silverware, china, glassware, and kitchen necessities. The wedding coordinator or volunteer meets them and inventories all rental items.

12:00 P.M. The florist appears and begins setting up flowers. Bouquets, boutonnieres, and corsages are delivered to the wedding party.

3:00 P.M. Members of the catering staff arrive to set the tables. They also set up and stock the bar and organize the kitchen.

4:00 P.M. The musicians come to set up equipment and conduct a sound check. The rest of the catering staff shows up to prepare hors d'oeuvres and start preparing for dinner.

5:45 P.M. The tables are set, the bar is ready, and the decor is in place for guests' arrival.

6:00 P.M. The bride and groom, wedding party, and guests begin to arrive at the reception location. The guests are greeted with hors d'oeuvres, cocktails, and music.

The bride and groom welcome guests in a receiving line (optional), and guests deliver gifts, sign the guest book, and pick up their seating cards (also optional).

7:00–7:45 P.M. The meal is announced, and the guests make their way into the dining area to find their seats. The parents or hosts of the reception may formally welcome everybody (especially if there was no receiving line). The best man makes a toast to the bride and groom,

followed by a response from the groom and sometimes the bride, and more toasts from other family or friends. The officiant blesses the marriage and gives thanks (optional).

The first course is served (or the buffet is opened), and music and dancing continue. The bride, groom, and parents may walk around and visit tables throughout the reception.

7:45–8:30 P.M. The first course is cleared; the couple dance their first dance, followed by the other members of the wedding party; the second course is served and cleared.

8:30–9:15 P.M. The main course is served and cleared. The musicians sound the cue for the start of the cake-cutting ceremony. Additional toasts are made while cake, dessert, and coffee are served. Music and dancing continue.

9:15–10:00 P.M. The bride tosses the bouquet, the groom tosses the garter, and the bride and groom slip away to change into their departure outfits for the honeymoon. While their guests continue dancing and enjoying the music, the bride and groom depart.

As the party winds down, the musicians stop playing, the bar closes, and the parents say good-bye to the guests.

10:15 P.M. The caterer, florist, musicians, and party-rental company break down their equipment and begin to clear out supplies.

The event coordinator or volunteer is the last to leave the site, after confirming that all rented items have been accounted for and returned.

Wedding Cake Switcheroo

Instead of a huge, fancy cake that serves all of your guests, ask your baker to make a smaller "display cake" with all the trimmings that's big enough to serve half the guests, and simpler sheet cakes to serve the other half. The display cake is cut and served after the cake-cutting ceremony; meanwhile, the sheet cakes are cut in the kitchen. This method reduces the expense of an enormous cake—and your guests will never know the difference.

and your relatives, and then make their way to the reception and start enjoying the festivities while you stay behind to have the photographs taken.

Here's a simple plan that will take the guesswork out of deciding who is supposed to stand where in the receiving line: The host of the wedding heads the line, and everybody else in the group follows to the left. If the parents of the bride are hosting, for instance, the mother would greet the guests first, followed by the father on her left. Next to him would be the mother of the groom, followed by the father of the groom, the bride herself, the groom, the honor attendant, and the best man.

Sometimes the fathers of the bride and groom step out of the receiving line to cir-culate in the crowd and receive congratulations, while the mothers remain, each standing next to her own child.

When the guests pass through the line, thank them for coming and then introduce them to any members of the receiving line they haven't met. Offer a handshake or a hug, whichever seems more appropriate. Don't worry if you happen to blank out on someone's name. Just smile, nod, and thank him or her for coming. Keep all of your greetings brief so guests don't have to wait very long. If the receiving line is at the reception site, make it more enjoyable for guests waiting in line by asking waiters to come by with hors d'oeuvres and drinks.

Special entrance for the bride and groom. This is a nice touch if you are having a sit-down lunch or dinner. Following the cocktails, when the meal is announced, everyone takes a seat except the bride and groom. Once all the guests are seated, the musicians announce your entrance and you proceed to the dance floor for your first dance. Save other special dances with parents or wedding party members until after the first course is cleared, about two hours into the reception.

Toasting. Traditionally the best man is the toastmaster. (If you aren't hiring musicians or a disc jockey, you can also ask the best man to be the master of ceremonies.) He gives the first toast to the new couple. Then the groom usually gives a response. It needn't be elaborate; a few simple but heartfelt words about his new bride and both sets of parents will suffice. The bride may want to respond, too. Parents, relatives, the wedding party, and close friends

can offer toasts as well. It is proper to stand when making or responding to a toast and to be seated when receiving one.

Some impromptu speeches are fine, but it's best to have an idea of who will be offering toasts and in what order. Once more, the best man can step in to simplify your life. Let him handle this task by contacting in advance anyone who may want to give a toast. He should advise them to limit speeches to three minutes or less.

Toward the end *of the reception, guests may shower you with spontaneous toasts as the champagne is poured. Enjoy it all—this is your one day to revel in the attention.*

rent one from an audiovisual company or a party-rental business, or have your site manager provide one.

Cake-cutting ceremony. As a symbol of fertility and good fortune, the wedding cake is thought to bestow good luck upon all those who take a bite. At a lunch or

The groom's response to the first toast needn't be elaborate; a few simple but heartfelt words will suffice.

Personal stories, fond memories, and funny anecdotes make for heartwarming toasts. Embarrassing stories are considered taboo, no matter how humorous they may be.

If your reception is very large, you may want to provide a cordless microphone so that the guests don't miss out on any of the toasting. You can ask the musicians to bring one with the rest of their equipment,

dinner reception, the cake is normally cut just before it is served; at a cocktail reception or tea, the bride and groom should cut it just after greeting guests.

The groom places his hand over the bride's, and together they cut a piece from the bottom tier of the cake. They feed one another that slice, with the bride taking the first bite. The bride then serves cake to

After the wedding cake is cut, *it is traditional to save a piece and freeze it to enjoy together on your first anniversary.*

the groom's parents, and the groom serves the bride's parents. One or both of the newlyweds offers a thank-you toast. The rest of the cake is then cut and served to the guests by the catering staff or by some preselected volunteers.

Tossing the bouquet and the garter. The lucky woman and man who catch these items are said to be the next in the crowd

to marry—though not necessarily to each other. If you choose to include these traditions, the bandleader or disc jockey first asks all the single women to gather for the bouquet toss just before the bride and groom slip out to change their outfits for travel. After the bouquet is caught, all the single men gather. The groom removes the bride's garter and tosses it to them.

Many brides want to hold on to their flowers as a remembrance. If you'd like to keep yours, you can have your bouquet and toss it, too, by using a second, stand-in arrangement. This bouquet is generally smaller and less expensive than the bridal one, and it doesn't have to come from the florist. Ask an aunt or close friend to make one from garden flowers.

Showering the newlyweds. Guests can cheer the newlyweds as they leave. Attendants provide birdseed or other material to toss (see page 99).

Give a Schedule to Key Participants

To make the reception flow smoothly, type up and distribute the schedule to all vendors and members of the wedding party. Appoint someone to ensure that things run according to plan— the wedding consultant, your caterer or site manager, or a trusted friend or relative who isn't in the wedding party.

ONE-DAY PLANNERS

Hire a wedding coordinator or party planner just to handle the wedding-day schedule. You'll rest easy knowing there's a pro guiding your wedding party and vendors, and ensuring that things run smoothly. You can even ask him or her to create the program of events and distribute it. As the last one to leave the reception, this point person assumes the responsibility of handling any loose ends.

Once you've got your schedule all set, hand it off to whoever is in charge—and then just forget about it. Concentrate on having fun and spending time with your guests, not on watching the clock.

PLANNING FOR GUESTS

---✳---

THERE'S NO DOUBT ABOUT IT—YOUR WEDDING RECEPTION, NO MATTER HOW SIMPLE, IS DESTINED TO BE A PARTY TO REMEMBER. YOUR GUESTS ARE SURE TO ENJOY THE WONDERFUL FOOD, MUSIC, AND AMBIENCE YOU'VE CREATED.

But there are a few practical details that you need to take care of for your guests' comfort—and your own peace of mind.

PARKING SOLUTIONS

If you've chosen a reception site that routinely handles large groups, parking will be a snap; such locations almost always offer ample parking for guests. Most hotels and clubs offer a valet parking service— either free or for an additional per-car charge. If your budget allows, include the extra cost in the contract; otherwise, let your guests pay for their own parking.

If your location does not have valet parking, ask the site manager how other parties have been accommodated there.

For weddings on a beach, in a park, or at another location not normally set up for parties, seek guidance from the parks-and-recreation department or from the manager of the space you rented. Chances are, a party has taken place there before and a parking solution was found.

If the site manager can't offer a simple solution, call a parking service. Look in the Yellow Pages under "Parking Attendant Service" or "Buses," or ask your wedding vendors for referrals.

Find out what the service offers as an alternative to traditional valet parking. Most provide shuttle service. They'll scout out nearby parking lots for the shuttle base and work out the costs. They'll also know

Avoid overcrowding your guests. Consider the size
of your tables before drawing up the seating plan.

how to check with the local government about a permit to reserve the parking on a street near your home.

If you can't afford a valet service, you may be tempted to consider hiring a teenage neighbor. That's really false economy, however. If anything should happen to a guest's car, you could be held responsible.

If you're arranging transportation for your guests from the ceremony to the site of the reception, or you're providing complimentary parking at a garage or parking lot, include the details on a card or map for your guests. The simplest way to let them know is to send an explanation as soon as you receive their R.S.V.P.

SEATING PLANS

Seating plans are meant to make your life easier, so don't be anxious about who sits where. Remember, at your wedding there's not a bad seat in the house. The general rule is that the more formal the occasion, the more specific the seating. For formal occasions, usually a table and a specific seat are designated. Accordingly, each of the guests would receive a seating card at the entrance, indicating the table number; place cards mark the seating at the tables. For semiformal affairs, just designate the table and let guests arrange themselves. At an informal reception, not even the tables need to be assigned—although you can still work out a seating plan if you want to. Sometimes the bride and groom are seated

Seating plans are meant to make your life easier, so don't be anxious about who sits where. Remember, there's not a bad seat in the house.

at a focal spot called the head table, or dais. For a simpler approach, don't bother setting up a specially decorated or raised table for this purpose. Just designate one of the regular tables for yourselves and other tables for your parents if you're not seating them with you. Place your table and your parents' in a central location, then assign the rest of the seating.

Ask your caterer or site manager how many guests can fit at each table. If you're renting your own tables, seat 8 guests at a 60-inch (152cm) round table, 10 guests at a 66-inch (168cm) round, and 12 guests at a 72-inch (183cm) round.

It's fine to mix and match table sizes to accommodate the number of guests you want to group at each table. The site manager should be able to provide a diagram

Plan a Children's Table

Make the tablecloth out of plain white butcher paper, and ask a friend or family member who is attending with children to bring crayons and markers, toys, and books to keep them busy. Ask a few volunteers to take turns chaperoning if you think the kids are likely to get restless.

EASY FAVORS

✳

THE FINISHING TOUCHES OF YOUR WEDDING are often the most fun. Send your guests away with a memento of your big day. Choose a small, personal gift that includes one of your favorite things. Make these simple favors yourself, or call in your wedding coordinator, attendants, or friends to help.

Fill an eclectic array *of small jars with romantic candy hearts. Finish them off by tying satin ribbon around the lids. These are perfect favors for a Valentine's Day wedding.*

Include your own *custom message in a fortune cookie placed in a tiny white take-out box. Fill the box with tissue. Order the cookies from a local baker.*

Dress up a candle *by tying a decorative ribbon around it and tucking a stem of dried flowers into the bow.*

Add real sparkle *to the festivities with a simple offering of sparklers and a matchbook tied together with shiny silver ribbon.*

Share your joy with every guest—present each with a small favor to commemorate your special day.

showing the placement of tables, or you can plot it out yourself on a piece of graph paper. Number the tables and write down who will be seated at each one. Here are a few guidelines to help you along:

◆ TRY TO SEAT OLDER GUESTS AWAY FROM THE BAND.

◆ SEAT GUESTS WHO SHARE SIMILAR INTERESTS TOGETHER, AND MIX IN OTHER PEOPLE THEY HAVEN'T MET.

◆ SEAT THE OFFICIANT AT ONE OF THE PARENTS' TABLES.

◆ SEAT TEENAGERS TOGETHER. THEY'LL HAVE MORE FUN THAT WAY.

GIVING FAVORS

A small favor to take home will remind your guests of the lovely event for years to come. Gather together your creative friends and family to brainstorm. Just keep in mind that the best favors come from your heart, and they do not have to be expensive or elaborate—they're merely symbolic expressions of affection.

A knotted ribbon is a charming favor that has roots in the past—party favors originated in the 16th century when knots

were cut off the bridal bouquet and given to guests to impart luck. To create these, make a simple knot in the same ribbon used for your bouquet and place it in a small envelope along with a printed message describing the tradition.

UNEXPECTED GUESTS

Life is always easier when you plan for the unexpected. If someone brings a guest you didn't invite to the reception, don't panic. Ask your honor attendant to handle it with your wedding coordinator or caterer.

A few adjustments will take care of the problem. Add another place setting next to the invited guest's seat. To prepare for this possibility in advance, if you are using seating and place cards, request that your stationer include a few additional blanks in your order. Before the wedding, give the extras to the caterer, coordinator, or honor attendant, who can fill in the extra guest's name. Don't worry about the handwriting on the new card. The unexpected guest will feel welcome no matter how the seating and place cards look.

GET UP AND DANCE

——— ✳ ———

MUSIC ELEVATES YOUR RECEPTION TO A TRUE CELEBRATION. SELECTING THE RIGHT SOUND TO FIT THE DAY'S MOOD CAN BE BOTH EASY AND INEXPENSIVE. START BY IDENTIFYING THE STYLE OF MUSIC YOU WANT.

Think about what's appropriate for the age range of your guests and what will keep everyone dancing. You have plenty to choose from: jazz (swing, progressive, or classic), big band, Broadway tunes, country and western, fifties sock hop, rock and roll (from the sixties or seventies), popular, or ethnic. Consider the style of your wedding. An elegant orchestra playing Glenn Miller tunes complements a formal party. A small but exquisite swing band is perfect for almost any occasion, as is a talented pianist who is also a vocalist.

You basically have three choices: live music, recorded music, or a combination of the two. A band is more expensive than a disc jockey and takes up more room. One way around the expense is to arrange to have recorded music played during cocktails and hire a band or orchestra to play for the rest of the reception. Find out if your site manager can play recorded music through an existing sound system. Tape a selection of your favorite tunes and put someone in charge of playing it.

Next, think about how you want to hire the entertainment. If you've already chosen musicians for the ceremony, then the simplest option is to use them for the reception, too. Ask your wedding consultant for advice, or consider hiring an entertainment consultant. Professionals often work with the same musicians for many events and have great contacts. Be very clear about how much you're willing to spend, and leave it up to them to offer you a plan within your budget.

After the wedding party *has had its turn, the dance floor opens up to all the guests. Choose music that will get everyone dancing.*

The Most Band for Your Buck

The price of a band is based on the number of musicians it includes. Today's technology allows a four-piece band to sound like a much larger group. With the help of synthesizers, drum machines, and computers, musicians can add percussion, strings, or horns without charging you for additional band members. Ask your bandleader about including this equipment.

HIRING A BAND

Finding a band can be as simple as calling the local musicians' union and getting a few names. You can also ask for referrals from radio stations, hotels, wedding vendors, family, friends, and colleagues.

If you can spare the time, plan a fun evening out with your wedding party or a group of friends, hopping from club to club to hear bands that might be appropriate for your reception.

When you research bands, ask how many musicians and vocalists it will take to produce enough sound to fill the room where you'll hold the reception, and have the bandleader provide a written quotation that outlines all the specifics. Also ask the band to handle such details as sound equipment and getting in touch with the location to see how it can meet the band's power and space requirements.

Specify the wardrobe of the band, too. If you don't want your bandleader making numerous announcements or sporadic comments during the festivities, make that clear up front. Provide the band with your special song requests, or ask for guidance in choosing the music for special dances. If the bandleader is to be your master of ceremonies as well, provide him or her with a complete schedule of events.

When hiring musicians, be sure they will bring recorded music to play during their breaks—or confirm that one musician will play while the others take a break.

If you have talented family and friends whom you would like to include in the entertainment, eliminate problems by confirming that the band is comfortable with these guest performers. Add these details to your schedule of events so everybody knows what's going on.

USING DISC JOCKEYS

Don't be turned off by the idea of hiring a disc jockey. Things have changed greatly since the days of the stereotypical guy who showed up in an open shirt and gold chains to play disco tunes. Today there are many professional DJs who offer continuous music specially tailored for your celebration and your personal tastes.

A DJ will come dressed however you specify and can even act as the master of ceremonies for the reception. You can pick a different style of music for each stage of the reception—why not choose fifties music for cocktails, switch to big-band sounds for mealtime, and move into contemporary or salsa for serious dancing?

Choose the music that best suits
the tone of your reception.

SPECIAL DANCES

One intriguing element that distinguishes wedding receptions from other parties is the ritual of the first few dances. These are easy to coordinate. The first dance begins with the bride and groom dancing to "their song" and is followed by some orchestrated switching of partners. (If the newlyweds already danced before dinner, they'll be invited back to the dance floor.)

The formula goes like this: The father of the bride cuts in about halfway through the song to dance with his daughter, while the groom dances with his new mother-in-law. After that, the bride dances with the father of the groom, the groom with his mother, and the bride's parents dance together. Then the bride dances with the best man, the groom with the honor attendant, and the groom's parents dance with each other. Grandparents, aunts and uncles, or siblings can substitute for parents.

It's OK for this first round of dancing to spill over into a couple of songs. The switching is determined by when the next person cuts in to dance with the bride.

Just tell the wedding party how the order goes. The rest of the wedding party is then invited to dance, followed by the remaining guests. You may want to include some appropriate ethnic dances that celebrate your new marriage and joint heritage.

Whatever style of entertainment you choose, don't worry about a perfect performance. You and your guests will be too busy having a good time to notice.

The Classic Ensemble

Hiring a band doesn't mean you need a stage full of musicians. The classic trio of piano, bass, and drums can provide almost any sound you're looking for. Tailor the playlist to the formality of your wedding. For a special touch, hire a vocalist to sing with your trio for an hour.

Your Big Getaway

※

Many couples choose to make their departure while their guests continue to party. If that's your plan, enjoy one last dance together after the cake cutting and the bouquet and garter toss.

Then give a good-bye toast and make a dash for your car amid a shower of rose petals, bubbles, or birdseed. If you are changing into a travel outfit, you should slip away with your attendants to change just before your last dance.

Some couples opt to stay to the end of their reception to soak up every last bit of the festivities. Staying until the end is recommended if you have many out-of-town guests attending. It affords a chance to offer a personal farewell to each one. Be sure to let everyone know if you're staying until the end, because some guests feel

obligated to wait for the bride and groom to depart before leaving. Mention your intention to stay when you offer a thank-you toast after the cake-cutting ceremony. Plan for the showering to take place sometime between the ceremony and reception. If the two of you are the first out the door, go to a private area and emerge when all are assembled and ready to shower you.

HOW TO TIP

Tipping some of the staff is customary, but you certainly don't want to think about that as your reception winds down. Figure

---

SIMPLE SOLUTIONS

GETTING TO YOUR HOTEL

Whether you stay at the reception until the very last song or make your getaway early, don't be stressed out over how to get to your hotel for the first night of your honeymoon. Arrange the transportation ahead of time. It's easy.

Simple

Hire a car or limousine to pick you up at the reception. Ask the hotel or your site manager for a referral. Hire a blast-from-the-past antique auto for a touch of character.

Simpler

Traditionally, the best man takes care of the bride and groom's transportation after the reception, so put yourselves in his hands and arrange for him to drive you to your hotel.

Simplest

Spend the first night or the entire honeymoon at the same hotel where you have your reception. No additional transportation is required—just walk to your room.

---

out all the tipping ahead of time, and give the wedding coordinator or host the right amounts in envelopes to distribute. Some vendors include gratuities in their invoice. Check with the caterer, banquet manager, and all other vendors to find out whether this is the case. You may want to give an additional tip for top-notch service.

Here's a guideline to appropriate tipping practices. For the wedding consultant, location manager, and florist: A gratuity is not usually expected, but you may want to give a small present and a thank-you note to them and to key members of their staff. Caterer, wait staff, and banquet or club manager: Give 15 to 20 percent of the bill if it's not included on the invoice. Parking attendants: Either the host pays the gratuity prior to the party or the guests tip as their cars arrive. If the host is prepaying, include this information along with your

If you've always dreamed *of making a dramatic exit, hire an old-fashioned carriage or vintage automobile for your getaway.*

invitation so your guests don't double-tip. Limousine driver: Give 15 to 20 percent if the tip is not included on the invoice. Musicians: Tipping is optional. You may want to give the bandleader 10 percent of the invoice to split among the musicians.

AFTER THE BIG EVENT

The reception is sometimes not the final wedding get-together. You could attend a postwedding brunch or informal party the day after the wedding, especially during long-weekend celebrations. It gives you another chance to visit with friends and family whom you don't see on a regular basis. Since everyone will most likely be all partied out, keep it simple and casual. Perhaps a family member or a friend will offer to host a gathering. If you are marrying in a hotel and many of the guests are staying over, negotiate to include a small brunch in your wedding package.

Before you leave for your honeymoon, take a moment to thank your parents for all their support. This doesn't require a big speech; a sincere thank-you, a small gift, and a note from the heart is all it really takes. (See page 52 for some gift ideas.) Send them a postcard from your honeymoon destination to let them know that you are having a wonderful time.

Be sure to let everyone know if you're staying until the end, because some guests may feel obligated to wait for your departure.

THE GREAT Escape

---*---

1 Keep on top of the **honeymoon** by planning it at the same time you start the other wedding tasks. **2** Check local **resorts** and hotels. You may even decide you'd rather stay in your own town. **3** Regardless of your final **destination,** book a nearby hotel room for your first night together. You'll be much more refreshed the next morning when it's time to embark. **4** Meet with several travel agents to find one who best understands the style of **getaway** you're looking for. **5** Find out if paying for a **car rental** with your credit card automatically insures you. **6** If you'll be traveling out of the country, obtain a small amount of **foreign currency** before you depart. That way you'll have taxi fare and money for tips when you arrive. **7** Tie up any loose ends when you return home. Send a **thank-you note** for every gift received and to each host of any parties given in your honor. **8** Create a wedding **time capsule.** Store invitations, favors, dried flowers from your bouquet, photographs, and your organizer together in a chest or trunk. ●

THE
HONEYMOON
AND BEYOND

PLANNING YOUR NEW LIFE TOGETHER

* —— ✳ —— *

The honeymoon is the perfect invention—a peaceful interlude that lets you bask in wedded bliss without the pressures of work or family getting in the way. Scheduling your first adventure together as husband and wife can be a stress-free process, whether you decide to embark on a round-the-world tour, hit mountain trails with pack llamas in tow, or sneak away to a hotel down the block.

A honeymoon offers a relaxed, intimate beginning to the rest of your lives together. It doesn't have to be elaborate or expensive. The trick to making it special is identifying what you both love doing as a couple. A travel agent can help you with the decision making and the details of planning. Save the fun stuff to do yourself, like arranging for that special bottle of champagne to be waiting in your room.

DESTINATIONS AND ITINERARIES

---✳---

THE FIRST STEP FOR EASY HONEYMOON PLANNING IS TO THINK ABOUT WHAT YOU BOTH ENJOY MOST: DO YOU PREFER MIXING SPORTS WITH LEISURE, FOCUSING ON SIGHTSEEING, OR JUST PLAIN RELAXING?

Do you want to escape to the country or explore the big city? What's best for you, a quaint inn or a luxury resort?

Answering these questions will help you focus on the perfect spot. You don't even have to leave town to have a great honeymoon. Check out local resorts and hotels, and ask concierges what kinds of activities they can tailor just for you.

To find ideas, flip through travel magazines, consult a travel agent, ask friends and family where they've spent their best vacations, and check out the Internet. As you come across great ideas, write them down to discuss with your fiancé. Keep on top of the honeymoon by scheduling it at the same time you start the other wedding tasks. If you still aren't sure how you want to spend your honeymoon, here are some categories to inspire you:

The sporting life. If both of you like to be active, take a vacation that lets you indulge in your favorite sports—hiking, biking, fishing, golf, tennis, river rafting, skiing, or horseback riding. Many resorts offer a host of facilities and equipment,

The best honeymoon involves
activities you both enjoy.

SIMPLE SOLUTIONS

PROTECTING YOUR LUGGAGE

TO IMPROVE THE ODDS OF RETRIEVING YOUR BAGS when you reach your airport destination, take a nonstop or direct flight. In your carry-on bags, keep an inventory of the items you pack, in case you must make an insurance claim.

Simple

Carry all your bags onto the plane. You'll have to pack light to accomplish this, but you'll be secure in the knowledge that there's no possibility your luggage will get lost.

Simpler

Check your larger bags. Tie luggage tags to handles and strap colored bands around the bags so you can recognize them immediately at the luggage carousel.

Simplest

Merely label checked luggage with your name and phone number. Make sure the tags are large enough to read easily, and attached securely so that they won't fall off.

all located on one property. Check with your credit card company's travel department or with a travel agent for suggestions.

Fantastic voyage. Sail away on a cruise that offers activities you are interested in. Luxurious yachts have spacious staterooms and fewer than 150 guests on board, and offer the privacy of candlelit dinners or the option of dancing with a crowd. Exotic destination cruises are the perfect way to take in several intriguing locations on one trip. Fitness fanatics can find cruise ships that provide workout facilities and spa cuisine. For the ultimate in relaxation, hop aboard a ship destined for the tropics. Sip fruit cocktails, lounge on deck, and visit the ports of call. Find a travel agency that specializes in cruises and describe what kind of trip you'd like to take.

Romantic roamings. Rent a convertible and head out on a road trip, stopping at

idyllic country inns along the way. Fill your days with picnics and shopping for antiques for your new home, and your evenings with romantic dinners and relaxation. Many auto clubs can help with the routing and accommodations.

Mountaintop hideaways. For the couple who loves nature, a cozy cabin and the beauty of the outdoors are a perfect match. If you're concerned you'll be too isolated, pick a spot that has plenty of activities close by. National and state parks are a great place to start.

Art adventure. Do painting and sculpture appeal to you? Build your itinerary around visits to the world's greatest art museums—or those of your own region. If European cities suit you, start in Paris and take the train to Venice, one of the most romantic and culturally rich cities in the world. For ultimate luxury, book

Off-Season Package Deals

The slow season for a resort can be the perfect time for you. Many tropical destinations are busiest when it's cold in other regions. During summer, prices can dip as much as 40 percent off the regular rates and often include meals, sightseeing tours, and a rental car. It's well worth investigating with a travel agent.

passage on the Orient Express. Or take a trip on this stellar train to some exotic cities throughout Southeast Asia.

Gourmets' delight. Good food and fine wine go hand in hand. For an extraordinary getaway, visit a region that's known for its wines. Enjoy sampling fine wines while indulging in superb cuisine. Bring home bottles of wine that require many years of aging; open them on anniversaries to come. You can browse through wine connoisseur and gourmet magazines for hints on the best spots.

Cosmopolitan chic. Play tourist in your own city. Stay in a hotel full of character, go out for romantic dinners (or have candlelit dinners in your room), enjoy theater shows, take long walks together, and do a little window shopping. Make sure that calls to the office are strictly off limits!

Casino action. Gamblers' havens are popular destinations for honeymooners. The casino complexes have it all: dancing, gambling, and glitzy cabaret shows in the evening, with resort-style living throughout the day. Hide away in your room or step out into exhilarating nightlife.

Tropical paradise. Spectacular sunsets, hammocks for two, and beaches, beaches, beaches—it's no wonder this is one of the most popular styles of honeymoon. Take midnight strolls barefoot along the shore, go scuba diving and snorkeling, drink piña coladas from coconuts, or do nothing at all! Ask your travel agent about package deals to resorts before deciding on which spot will be the best for you.

Riding the rails. You can go exploring on a cross-country train journey. Reserve a fabulous compartment and take in panoramic scenery as the train roars through the countryside. Hop off to stay in quaint hotels along the way.

PLANNING THE TRIP

Decide how involved you want to be in making the travel arrangements. Do you want to spend time surfing the Net for destinations and making your own phone calls to airlines and hotels, or would you rather enlist the help of a travel agency? Agents can guide you to the latest and greatest destinations. Let them do the research on lodgings, restaurants, activities, airfares, car rentals, and train timetables. They'll also advise you on passports, travel visas, and inoculations.

Agents often collect their fees from the airline, resort, or cruise line, but sometimes the customer will pay a commission. Ask up front to determine if the agency will cost you. Check with several travel

No matter where you go, your honeymoon is bound to be blissful.

agents to find one who best understands the style of getaway you are looking for—even if you're staying in your own city.

No matter where you're heading, plan to spend the first night at a nearby hotel. After the festivities, you'll probably be too tired to hop on a plane or drive long distances. You'll be much more refreshed for the journey the next morning.

If you'll be traveling out of the country, it's helpful to obtain a small amount of foreign currency before your departure. That way you'll have taxi fare and money for tips when you arrive. Try to book non-stop flights. Next best is a direct flight, which stops along the way but allows you to stay in the plane. Avoid connecting flights, which involve changing planes. If you have a frequent-flier program, check for mileage awards you can cash in for a free flight, a rental car, or a hotel room. Also check with your credit card company before renting any car: If you pay for the rental with a credit card, it may cover collision and personal liability (you need both), so you can skip rental agency insurance.

Take along all your confirmation documentation in case there are discrepancies upon arrival. If you find that your ocean-view hotel room faces a wall, you'll have written proof of what you reserved.

It never hurts to mention that you're honeymooners. You'll often be pampered with special treatment, free upgrades, or complimentary champagne.

Check Travel Advisories

If you're concerned about your personal safety at a destination, check with the personnel at the appropriate government agency. They can advise you of countries with hazardous conditions, health risks, and hostile local environments. Some newspapers also feature a section advising on world travel.

COMING HOME

———— ✳ ————

TO START YOUR NEW LIFE TOGETHER, DON'T FORGET THE TIME-HONORED RITUAL OF HAVING THE GROOM CARRY THE BRIDE OVER THE THRESHOLD— ORIGINALLY THOUGHT TO PROTECT HER FROM LURKING DEMONS.

If you're not too exhausted after your honeymoon, invite a few guests over to help organize your wedding gifts and reminisce about the celebration.

Over the next couple of weeks, you'll have a few loose ends to tie up. But don't worry. These tasks are easy compared with planning the wedding.

Writing thank-you notes. Send a note to everyone who gave you a gift and to each person who hosted a shower or engagement party (see the gift log on page 135).

Selecting photographs. Your photographer will be sending you proofs of all the photos taken at the wedding. When you choose photos to have enlarged for your album, try to include a variety of posed and candid shots. You may want to select a picture of the two of you to send out with your thank-you notes.

Assembling your own photo albums. Put photographs from prewedding parties and get-togethers in albums as soon as you can. These events were as much a part of the wedding as the formal celebration, so why not keep mementos of them accessible instead of filing them away?

Preserving your wedding gown. Choose a reputable dry cleaner that will also preserve your wedding gown in a box after cleaning it. (You can ask for a referral when you purchase your gown.)

Creating a wedding time capsule. After planning such an exceptional event, you may want to preserve keepsakes, photos, and your trusty planning binder all together in one spot. The easiest place to store everything is in a chest or a trunk (some, sold for this purpose, even have a special compartment for your gown). Put everything related to the wedding inside: invitations to prewedding parties, dried flowers from the bouquet, a favor from the reception, your wedding journal, and notes the two of you wrote to each other. Years from now you'll enjoy a romantic evening together looking back on all the fun.

Preserve Your Gown Yourself

Soon after your gown has been cleaned, take it off the hanger and fold it with layers of acid-free tissue (ask a dry cleaner where to buy it). Wrap the gown with natural muslin and store it in a dark, dry place. A chest or drawer lined in cedar will keep moths away. Take the dress out annually and refold it to avoid setting the creases.

CHECKLISTS

AND RESOURCES

INFORMATION FOR WEDDING PLANNERS

——————*

The checklists in this chapter will help you keep on top of every wedding detail. They include a countdown checklist, a worksheet for thank-you notes, and a list that spells out the duties of the best man and honor attendant.

There are also lists of questions for caterers, musicians, photographers, and other wedding vendors—even the travel agent to help you plan the perfect honeymoon getaway. These lists will help you hire experienced wedding professionals and give you the peace of mind that comes from knowing there'll be no unpleasant surprises on your special day.

Finally, whether you're simply looking for more guidance or for a particular item, there are additional resources, including publications, Internet sites, organizations, and suppliers of everything from table linens to limousine service.

If you follow the tips and use the checklists and resources, you're certain to have the kind of celebration you want.

CONTACT LIST

IMPORTANT NUMBERS AT YOUR FINGERTIPS

---*---

KEEP IN ONE PLACE THE PHONE NUMBERS FOR EVERYONE ON YOUR TEAM. INCLUDE ALL NUMBERS, IF POSSIBLE: HOME, OFFICE, MOBILE, AND FAX. FOR BUSINESSES, NOTE HOURS OF BUSINESS AND AN ALTERNATE CONTACT PERSON.

PROFESSIONAL SERVICES

Wedding consultant_____

_____

_____

_____

Stationer_____

_____

_____

_____

Florist_____

_____

_____

_____

Caterer_____

_____

_____

_____

Entertainment consultant or bandleader

_____

_____

Party-supply company_____

_____

_____

Photographer_____

_____

_____

Videographer_____

_____

_____

_____

WARDROBE

Bridal salon_____

_____

_____

_____

Formal-wear shop_____

_____

_____

_____

WEDDING PARTY & HELPERS

Honor attendant_____

_____

Best man_____

_____

Bridal attendants_____

_____

_____

_____

_____

_____

_____

_____

Groomsmen_____

_____

_____

_____

_____

_____

_____

Bride's parents_____

_____

_____

_____

Groom's parents_____

_____

_____

Flower girl_____

Ring bearer_____

CEREMONY & RECEPTION

Ceremony location_____

_____

_____

Officiant_____

_____

Reception location_____

_____

TRANSPORTATION & PARKING

To ceremony_____

_____

To reception_____

_____

To hotel_____

_____

To airport_____

_____

HONEYMOON CONTACTS

Travel agent_____

_____

_____

Airline_____

_____

_____

_____

Hotel_____

_____

_____

_____

Cruise line_____

_____

_____

_____

Car rental agency_____

_____

_____

BOOKING A CEREMONY SITE

FINDING THE PLACE THAT SUITS YOU BEST

———— ✳ ————

START THE PROCESS BY PHONING AS MANY PLACES AS YOU CAN. ONCE YOU'VE NARROWED DOWN YOUR CHOICES TO THREE OR FOUR, MAKE ON-SITE VISITS AND MEET THE OFFICIANT WHO WILL BE MARRYING YOU. HERE'S WHAT TO ASK:

- Are we required to be members of the congregation in order to marry?

- Is premarital counseling required? If so, for how many sessions?

- Do you have restrictions on interfaith marriages? If you don't, do you permit both clerics to officiate?

- May we use our own words for our vows or in the ceremony?

- Are there certain religious holidays on which weddings may not take place?

- Are there any other ceremonies taking place on the same day as ours?

- Do you have attire, music, decorating, or photography restrictions?

- Do you have a piano or organ on site? If so, is there an additional fee to use it?

- Do you have a music director or organist to assist with music selections?

- Who is my contact at the site?

- Do you provide any decorative elements such as an aisle runner, floral containers, or candles? If so, what is the fee?

- Are there any restrictions on having a candlelit ceremony?

- May we scatter flower petals down the center aisle instead of using a runner?

- Are there restrictions on showering us with flowers as we leave the ceremony? If it's permitted, do you have a crew to take care of the cleanup?

- Are there facilities where the bridal party can dress, and which include electrical outlets, mirrors, and powder rooms?

- How many people will the space accommodate comfortably?

- Do you have appropriate access and rest rooms for handicapped guests?

- Is parking available nearby?

- What are the site's use fees and how many hours does that include?

SELECTING A RECEPTION SITE

SO LITTLE TIME, SO MANY SITES TO SEE

———— ✳ ————

OF COURSE YOU WANT TO FIND A BEAUTIFUL SITE THAT MATCHES THE STYLE OF WEDDING YOU'VE ALWAYS DREAMED OF HAVING. CALL AROUND FIRST, THEN NARROW DOWN YOUR CHOICES FOR A FEW ON-SITE VISITS.

- What is the fee, what does it include, and for how many hours?

- Do you charge an overtime fee?

- How much is the deposit? Do you refund if we cancel or move the date?

- How many guests can the space accommodate, seated or standing?

- How many rest rooms are available? Do they accommodate handicapped guests?

- Can you provide tables, chairs, linens, serving ware, heaters, lights, a dance floor? If so, is there an additional fee?

- Do you have a kitchen? Is it fully equipped? If not, do you have limits on the type of equipment we bring?

- Can we bring in an outside caterer?

- Can we provide the liquor? If so, must we pay for liability insurance and corkage fees?

- Do you have a piano on site? Is there an additional fee to use it?

- Does the location have a sound system? If so, what are the details and fees?

- Can the location accommodate both the ceremony and the reception?

- What is the best backup plan for an outdoor event in case of bad weather?

- Is the gratuity included in your fee? If not, what percentage should we add?

Ask now, avoid surprises later.

QUESTIONS FOR PLANNERS

THE RIGHT WEDDING PLANNER IS WORTH EVERY PENNY

---※---

WEDDING CONSULTANTS CAN BE A GODSEND FOR THE BUSY COUPLE. THEY DO ALL THE LEGWORK AND INVOLVE YOU IN THE FINAL DECISIONS. ASK LOTS OF QUESTIONS BEFORE YOU CHOOSE THE PLANNER WHO'S RIGHT FOR YOU.

◆ Do you do all types or do you specialize in a particular style of wedding?

◆ How many weddings have you coordinated that are similar to ours in scope, budget, and atmosphere?

◆ Do you have a portfolio we can look through to see what you've done?

◆ Do you always handle the entire wedding, or can we hire you to do specific tasks? If so, which tasks are best?

◆ Will you oversee the rehearsal?

◆ What is your fee structure and is it flexible according to our needs? Do you charge a flat fee, an hourly fee, or a percentage of the wedding's total cost?

◆ Do you use only certain vendors, and do you receive commissions from them?

◆ Will you negotiate all contracts and secure the best prices?

◆ Can you purchase items wholesale (favors, flowers, napkins, and so on)?

◆ Can you advise us of all deadlines (guest count, flowers, decor elements) and help us make decisions relating to them?

◆ Will you generate the schedule of events and lists of contacts?

◆ Can you take care of organizing the invitation list and addresses and act as a liaison with the stationer?

◆ Can you help us select the groom's and groomsmen's attire and coordinate tuxedo or jacket rentals?

◆ Do you have any suggestions for the bride's and bridesmaids' attire?

◆ Will you help us put together the order of the procession and recession?

◆ Will you be present the day of our wedding to run the ceremony and reception? Will you stay until the end?

◆ Can you coordinate the wedding we've described and keep us within budget?

◆ Can you help us cut costs when needed?

QUESTIONS FOR FLORISTS

FROM CORSAGES TO CENTERPIECES: WHAT TO ASK

———— ✳ ————

Florists can be key when it comes to transforming the wedding and reception locations. They'll also provide your bouquets and boutonnieres. Asking targeted questions will put you on the right track.

- How many weddings do you do per year?

- Do you have a portfolio that we can look through for ideas?

- What is the maximum number of weddings you book for the same weekend?

- Do you offer party-planning services? If so, can you explain these services?

- Will you set up the centerpieces and various arrangements or just drop them off? Is there a delivery fee or an extra setup charge?

- Will you show us a mockup of our centerpieces or any other elements? If so, is there an extra charge?

- Can you show us examples of your most popular style of bouquet, boutonniere, corsage?

- If you use plastic bouquet holders, what do you use to cover the holders?

- How do we protect the flowers from wilting on hot days?

- Can you provide props, urns, and plant and tree rental services? If so, what is available and how much are the fees?

- Are you willing to share the floral responsibilities with the wedding party? If so, how would you divide it up?

- Are you familiar with our ceremony and reception locations? If not, will you walk through them ahead of time?

- How far in advance will you arrive at our ceremony and reception locations? How do you ensure the flowers last?

- How do you calculate your fee? Is it a flat rate, or is the fee flexible according to the scope of our needs?

- Does your fee include both your services and the price of all the flowers? Or do you itemize these separately?

- Are you willing to work within our budget? Does it seem realistic?

- Can we meet you at one of your wedding setups to see how you work?

QUESTIONS FOR CATERERS

A DELICIOUS MEAL IS THE BACKBONE OF YOUR EVENT

---- ✳ ----

CATERERS ARE AMONG THE PROFESSIONALS MOST COMMONLY HIRED FOR A WEDDING RECEPTION. THEY CAN PROVIDE JUST THE MEAL OR HANDLE EVERYTHING FROM SETUP TO CLEANUP. ASK ABOUT ALL THEIR SERVICES.

◆ Do you specialize in a particular type of cuisine or style of menu?

◆ How many events will you book for the same date or weekend as our wedding?

◆ Can you provide everything for the party, from linens to entertainment?

◆ Can we pick which services we wish to utilize? Do you have packages?

◆ Does your bid include a tasting for our menu? How many items can we taste?

◆ Can we meet you at one of your party setups to see how you work?

◆ Are you familiar with the site we have chosen? If so, are the kitchen facilities adequate? If not, will you walk through the site to establish what is required?

◆ Do you provide the staff, including bartenders and cleanup crew? If so, how will they be dressed?

◆ For a seated reception, how many waiters and bus people will you provide?

◆ If we provide the wedding cake from an outside baker, will you charge a service fee to cut and serve it?

◆ Can we provide our own liquor and have your staff serve it? If so, will you charge a corkage or service fee?

◆ Will you be using all fresh ingredients? Do you ever use frozen foods? How far in advance will you cook the meal?

◆ If I hire your services well in advance, will the fees be subject to increase if you change your prices down the road?

◆ Will you inform us and ask for our written approval before you make any food substitutes to our menu?

◆ Who will be on-site and in charge the day of our wedding? Will it be the representative we deal with throughout the wedding, or someone new?

◆ Is the gratuity included in your fee? Do the gratuities get passed to the staff? If so, what is the percentage and on what is the charge based?

QUESTIONS FOR PHOTOGRAPHERS

WEIGHING THE POSITIVES AND THE NEGATIVES

———— ✳ ————

W HEN IT COMES TO A PHOTOGRAPHER, YOUR CHOICE DEPENDS ON YOUR
TASTE AND BUDGET. EXAMINING THE WORK OF THREE OR FOUR PROFES-
SIONALS WILL HELP YOU NARROW YOUR OPTIONS.

◆ Can we review a complete shoot and
a finished album from a wedding that
had a similar location and guest count?

◆ Do you have a particular style or
approach when shooting a wedding?

◆ Can you work in both black-and-white
and color? Does the cost change?

◆ What is the balance you use between
posed and candid shots?

◆ What happens if your equipment jams?
Do you bring backup equipment?

◆ Will the photographer we meet with
be the one to shoot the wedding?
Is the cost of an assistant included?

◆ Will there be another photographer on
call in case of illness or an emergency?

◆ Do you charge by the roll, the hour,
or the print, or can we purchase an
all-inclusive package?

◆ If you charge by the hour, is there
a point where you charge overtime?

◆ Do you charge for travel time?

◆ How many rolls of film will you
be shooting at our wedding, and can
we purchase the negatives?

◆ Have you worked in the past at the
location we have selected?

◆ Will you stop by the rehearsal to
become familiar with the ceremony
and the participants?

◆ If we give you a shot list, will you be
able to take all the photographs specified, in addition to the ones you plan
to take? What is the maximum?

◆ How long after the wedding will we
receive our proofs? How long after we
select from the proofs will we receive
the album or prints?

◆ If we don't buy the negatives, how long
will you keep them on file? Do you also
keep contact sheets on file?

◆ What was the most difficult wedding
you've shot? What made it so difficult?

QUESTIONS FOR VIDEOGRAPHERS

FINDING A PRO WHO'LL FOCUS ON THE BIG PICTURE

———— ✳ ————

SOMETIMES A PHOTOGRAPHER AND A VIDEOGRAPHER WHO WORK TOGETHER WILL OFFER A PACKAGE DEAL. OTHERWISE, FIND A VIDEOGRAPHER ON YOUR OWN. ASK TO VIEW SAMPLE VIDEOS OF OTHER WEDDINGS.

◆ How many wedding videos do you do a month? Do you have any experience shooting home weddings?

◆ What kind of video equipment do you use? Is it professional, or something that we might own?

◆ How will you capture the audio? Can you wire the officiant with a cordless microphone? Other alternatives?

◆ May we view the raw footage as well as the finished video of a wedding similar in location, size, and style to ours?

◆ Can you tell us about the different styles of shooting and editing video (one camera versus multiple cameras, editing versus no editing)? What do you think is the best approach?

◆ What will the finished video of our wedding look like? How long will it be? Will it have any graphics, and can it include a photographic montage for the ending?

◆ What kind of packages do you sell? Do they include the master tape?

◆ How many copies of the finished video are included in the fee?

◆ What happens if your equipment jams or becomes inoperative? Will you have backup equipment on site?

◆ Will you attend the rehearsal to get a feel for the ceremony?

◆ Who will be shooting the video?

◆ How much experience does this videographer have? Can we meet him or her before the ceremony?

◆ How many hours of coverage does your fee include? What is considered overtime, and how much is that fee?

◆ Have you ever shot a wedding at our ceremony and reception locations?

◆ How long after the wedding will we receive the finished video?

◆ Can you describe what elements make a fantastic wedding video? What makes an uninteresting video?

QUESTIONS FOR MUSICIANS

HOW TO FIND HARMONY WHEN HIRING BANDS

———— ✷ ————

WHETHER YOU'RE A LITTLE BIT COUNTRY, A LITTLE BIT ROCK AND ROLL, OR SOMEWHERE IN BETWEEN, ASKING LOTS OF QUESTIONS IS THE BEST WAY TO BE COMFORTABLE WITH THE MUSICIANS YOU CHOOSE.

FOR THE CEREMONY

◆ Are you familiar with the location that we have chosen for our ceremony? If so, what type of music has worked well there in the past?

◆ Can we use taped music during our ceremony? Are you willing to help us select the songs?

◆ What are the most effective classical instruments to use (organ, piano, string trio, classic quartet)?

◆ Can you provide soloists? If so, may we hear their demo tapes or attend one of their performances?

◆ Will rehearsals be required if you perform with the church's musicians? If so, will there be an extra charge to cover these rehearsals?

◆ Who will the actual musicians be? Will you replace them only with our written approval?

◆ What music do you recommend for the processional and recessional?

FOR THE RECEPTION

◆ Do you have professional equipment?

◆ Do you provide your own sound system?

◆ Can you give us a proposed song list? Can we select the music?

◆ Will the bandleader or DJ act as master of ceremonies? Can we request that there be no chitchat between songs or that it be kept to a minimum?

◆ What will the musicians or DJ be wearing? Will they wear tuxedos?

◆ How often will you take breaks? Will there be recorded music or one person playing during breaks?

◆ Can a few of the musicians play during cocktails? Is there an extra charge or can this be included in the price?

◆ Are we supposed to provide meals for the musicians or DJ?

◆ Is there a performance we can attend prior to booking?

QUESTIONS FOR STATIONERS

MAKING SURE YOU GET THE WRITE STUFF

———————— ✳ ————————

WHEN LOOKING FOR A STATIONERY PROVIDER, GO WITH AN EXPERIENCED ESTABLISHMENT SUCH AS A CARD STORE, DEPARTMENT STORE, OR STATIONER. WHEN IN DOUBT ABOUT STATIONERY, MAKE A CONSERVATIVE DECISION.

◆ What is the average number of orders that you take in a given month for wedding invitations?

◆ Will you explain the different types of invitations—engraved, thermographed, printed, and so on?

◆ How many different styles of invitations do you offer? What are the price levels?

◆ What is your idea of the ultimate wedding invitation?

◆ Do you keep samples from past orders? May we see them?

◆ Are your sample invitations made of the same quality of paper stock as the invitations we will receive?

◆ Do you offer a discount if we order everything at the same time: thank-you notes, personal stationery, seating cards, and place cards?

◆ Can you help us with the proper wording and etiquette when we're ready to start addressing the envelopes?

◆ Do you have a calligrapher who can address envelopes and make out seating and place cards? What will it cost? Can it be done with a computer instead of by hand? What will that cost?

◆ What is the most economical invitation and response card you offer?

◆ Will you provide us with a proof of our invitation? If so, will there be an additional fee for that?

◆ If there is a spelling error, who pays to correct it?

◆ Will you put the place cards and seating cards in alphabetical order?

◆ How long will it take to receive the invitations after ordering them?

◆ Will you order special stamps for us from the post office?

◆ Will you mail the invitations if we hand-address them? If so, will you request that they be hand-canceled at the post office?

GIFT AND THANK-YOU LOG

A FILL-IN-THE-BLANKS TEMPLATE FOR TRACKING GIFTS

———— ✳ ————

STAY ON TOP OF THANK-YOU NOTES BY RECORDING A LITTLE INFORMATION ABOUT EACH GIFT AS YOU RECEIVE IT. THIS LOG CAN GET YOU STARTED. JUST PLACE IT ON THE PHOTOCOPIER AND MAKE AS MANY DUPLICATES AS YOU NEED.

Name and address of sender:_____
_____
_____
_____

Description of gift:_____
_____

Thoughts regarding gift:_____
_____

Store purchased at:_____
_____

Date received:_____

Date thank-you note sent:_____

Name and address of sender:_____
_____
_____
_____

Description of gift:_____
_____

Thoughts regarding gift:_____
_____

Store purchased at:_____
_____

Date received:_____

Date thank-you note sent:_____

Name and address of sender:_____
_____
_____
_____

Description of gift:_____
_____

Thoughts regarding gift:_____
_____

Store purchased at:_____
_____

Date received:_____

Date thank-you note sent:_____

Name and address of sender:_____
_____
_____
_____

Description of gift:_____
_____

Thoughts regarding gift:_____
_____

Store purchased at:_____
_____

Date received:_____

Date thank-you note sent:_____

FINDING A TRAVEL AGENT

LOCATING ONE WHO UNDERSTANDS WHAT YOU WANT

---✳---

A TRAVEL AGENT CAN SIMPLIFY THE DECISION OF WHERE IN THE WORLD TO GO ON YOUR HONEYMOON. FOR A DREAM VACATION, FIND AN AGENT WHO SPECIALIZES IN HONEYMOONS RATHER THAN BUSINESS OR TOUR TRAVEL.

- What kind of travel do you specialize in?

- What percentage of your business is generated from honeymoon travel?

- Is your agency a member of any professional organizations?

- Do you charge commissions on any of your services?

- Can you tell us what you think makes for a dream honeymoon?

- Will you explain various options based on our budget and length of getaway?

- What kinds of all-inclusive packages do you recommend and why? What are the drawbacks, if any?

- Can you explain off-season rates and tell us where it will be off-season when we want to go on our honeymoon? Will it be raining or too hot or cold (or buggy) for us to enjoy ourselves?

- What can we expect the weather to be like where we're going?

- Will you assist us with all travel documents and requirements?

- What kind of activities and facilities does the hotel/resort/cruise line you are recommending have?

- Can you explain the various styles of cruises? Have you ever been on one? If so, what was your experience?

- If we will be traveling by air, will you request special meals, confirm our seat assignments, and deliver our tickets and boarding passes to us?

- Will we be able to cash in our frequent-flier miles for travel tickets, hotel rooms, and rental cars?

- Will either our tickets or our hotel reservations be nonrefundable?

- What type of travel insurance is appropriate? Is it included when we charge our trip or tickets with a credit card?

- What is the best way for us to save money when booking our honeymoon?

HONEYMOON PACKING

GATHERING YOUR GETAWAY GEAR

———— ✳ ————

DON'T PUT OFF PACKING UNTIL THE LAST MINUTE, WHEN YOUR MIND IS ON OTHER WEDDING DETAILS. MOST OF THESE ITEMS ARE EASY TO COMPILE EARLY ON. ONE THING YOU'LL DEFINITELY WANT TO FORGET: YOUR ALARM CLOCK!

CARRY-ON LUGGAGE

- ☐ Airline or train tickets
- ☐ Passports
- ☐ Wallet, address book
- ☐ Driver's license
- ☐ Credit cards
- ☐ Traveler's checks
- ☐ Cash or local currency
- ☐ Confirmation and phone numbers for hotel, car rental, airline
- ☐ Prescription drugs
- ☐ Toiletries
- ☐ Spare eyeglasses
- ☐ Jewelry
- ☐ Camera, film
- ☐ House and car keys
- ☐ Change of clothing
- ☐ Sexy lingerie

TOILETRIES

- ☐ Shampoo, conditioner, shower cap
- ☐ Hair dryer, curling iron
- ☐ Soap, skin-care products
- ☐ Toothbrush, toothpaste
- ☐ Tweezers, manicure/pedicure kit
- ☐ Pain relievers
- ☐ Backup prescriptions
- ☐ Mouthwash
- ☐ Deodorant
- ☐ Razor
- ☐ Perfume or cologne, makeup

THE COMFORT ZONE

- ☐ Comfortable walking shoes
- ☐ Favorite jeans
- ☐ Knit clothing
- ☐ Versatile blazer

FOR BEACH LOVERS

- ☐ Swimsuits
- ☐ T-shirts, cover-ups
- ☐ Shorts
- ☐ Sunblock, hats
- ☐ Sunglasses
- ☐ Sandals or thongs
- ☐ Beach tote
- ☐ Novels, magazines
- ☐ Insect spray

Pack in advance to avoid stress.

PLANNING CHECKLIST

———— * ————

PLANNING YOUR WEDDING CAN BE DONE EFFICIENTLY BY USING THIS CHECK-LIST TO BREAK DOWN TASKS. DON'T WORRY IF YOU HAVE LESS THAN SIX MONTHS FOR PLANNING—JUST GATHER YOUR TEAM AND GET STARTED.

6 TO 12 MONTHS BEFORE

☐ Announce your engagement to family and friends.

☐ Discuss the style of wedding the two of you envision.

☐ Discuss among the two of you and both sets of parents how wedding expenses will be shared or divided.

☐ Choose an honor attendant and your bridesmaids.

☐ Choose a best man, groomsmen, and ushers (if necessary).

☐ Register for wedding gifts.

☐ Select a wedding date.

☐ Order the bridal gown; select dresses and accessories for the bridesmaids.

☐ Meet with officiant and fiancé to discuss ceremony.

☐ Discuss honeymoon plans.

4 TO 6 MONTHS BEFORE

☐ Assemble a binder to be used as your wedding organizer.

☐ Select ceremony and reception sites.

☐ Shop for wedding rings.

☐ Complete your guest list and ask your parents to do the same.

☐ Order attire for groom and groomsmen.

☐ Interview and hire professionals.

☐ Send out "save the date" cards if you set your date far in advance or if it falls during a holiday season.

☐ Reserve rental equipment if you're handling rentals yourself.

☐ Delegate transportation arrangements.

☐ Determine requirements for marriage license. Arrange for physical exam or blood test, if needed.

☐ Reserve hotel room for wedding night if you're not departing on honeymoon immediately after reception.

☐ Choose wedding favors. Ask honor attendant, wedding consultant, or stationer for assistance.

COMPLETE TASKS WITH EACH VENDOR:

☐ *Wedding consultant.* Discuss consultant's responsibilities.

☐ *Stationer.* Order invitations and all other stationery. Contact and reserve calligrapher, if desired.

☐ *Caterer.* Discuss and choose menu. Select other services to be provided.

☐ *Baker.* Order the cake if the caterer is not providing it.

☐ *Florist.* Order floral arrangements, bouquets, boutonnieres, and corsages.

☐ *Photographer.* Give shot list and discuss style of photography.

- [ ] *Videographer.* Discuss various styles and approaches of wedding videos and express your preferences.
- [ ] *Entertainment consultant or bandleader.* Select style of music for ceremony and reception. Compile a list of music for both. Attend performances of band prior to the wedding.

2 MONTHS BEFORE

- [ ] Address invitations.
- [ ] Send out invitations (6 to 8 weeks before the wedding).
- [ ] Check on vendors' progress and confirm arrangements with each one.
- [ ] Select gifts for each other, attendants, parents, and other helpers.
- [ ] Pick up rings and make sure they fit.
- [ ] Select readings, poems, or prayers for ceremony. To allow practice time, give copies to those who will be reading.
- [ ] If writing all or a part of your vows, begin to put them together.
- [ ] Stay on top of thank-you notes. Try to write them as you receive gifts.
- [ ] Confirm transportation arrangements and honeymoon plans.
- [ ] Work on favors if you or the wedding party are making them.

I MONTH BEFORE

- [ ] Check final details with all vendors.
- [ ] Have your final fitting for the gown. Bring shoes and hair accessories to confirm that the match is perfect.
- [ ] Send out additional invitations as you receive regrets.

- [ ] Work on seating plan.
- [ ] Meet with officiant to finalize the plans for the ceremony.
- [ ] Make arrangements for the rehearsal and rehearsal dinner
- [ ] Organize going-away outfit and clothing for honeymoon.
- [ ] Schedule final hair trimming.
- [ ] Plan transportation to the ceremony and the reception.

2 WEEKS BEFORE

- [ ] Check in with vendors as needed.
- [ ] Pick up marriage license with fiancé.
- [ ] Pick up wedding gown. Confirm that you have something old, something new, something borrowed, and something blue to wear.
- [ ] Practice hairstyle with headpiece, either by yourself or with a stylist.
- [ ] Schedule makeup trial run or practice.
- [ ] Begin writing seating and place cards or delegate this task to calligrapher, stationer, or attendants.
- [ ] Compose reception toasts.

I WEEK BEFORE

- [ ] Check in with vendors as needed.
- [ ] Confirm seating plan and give caterer final guest count.
- [ ] Finish writing seating and place cards.
- [ ] Assign wedding-day duties to your attendants and helpers.
- [ ] Pack for honeymoon.
- [ ] Attend rehearsal and rehearsal dinner.
- [ ] Create checklist of all items you will be bringing to ceremony and reception.

WEDDING DAY CHECKLIST

MAKING THE BIG DAY GO SMOOTHLY

———— ✳ ————

THE BIG DAY'S FINALLY HERE, AND YOU'RE AFRAID YOU WON'T REMEMBER EVERYTHING. RELAX. IT'S ALL HERE. JUST DON'T TRY TO DO IT ALL YOURSELF—THIS IS THE TIME TO DELEGATE WHATEVER TASKS YOU CAN.

ON THE WEDDING DAY

☐ Have breakfast with attendants, close family, or a few friends.

☐ Touch base with wedding consultant if you hired one.

☐ Before dressing, take a nice, relaxing bubble bath or enjoy a massage.

☐ Give groom's ring to honor attendant to hold for ceremony.

☐ Give bride's ring to best man to hold for the ceremony.

☐ Give officiant's fee to best man in sealed envelope.

☐ Have luggage and honeymoon documents taken to the reception location.

☐ Collect bridal bouquet and emergency kit (sewing, aspirin, and so forth) to bring to ceremony.

☐ Bring marriage license to ceremony.

☐ Pin on the boutonniere.

☐ Give gift to parents and thank them for their help and support.

BEFORE THE CEREMONY

☐ Confirm that chairs are set up and that all elements of the decor have been properly arranged.

☐ Confirm that musicians arrived on time—show them their setup area.

☐ Confirm that attendants and groomsmen have arrived at ceremony location, and distribute flowers and boutonnieres.

☐ Confirm that officiant has arrived at ceremony location.

☐ Confirm that photographer and/or videographer have arrived.

☐ Have honor attendant and best man sign the wedding certificate as witnesses.

BEFORE THE RECEPTION

☐ Ensure that the guest chairs, tables, and buffets have been set up and arranged according to plan.

☐ Confirm that guest tables are set with specified elements, such as specialty linens, place cards, and favors.

☐ Confirm that all decor elements have arrived and are in place.

☐ Confirm that caterer and/or bartender have arrived at reception location.

☐ Confirm that wedding cake has arrived at reception location.

☐ Confirm that musicians have arrived for setup and sound check.

☐ Confirm that a microphone (preferably cordless) is available for toasts.

☐ Confirm that the photographer and/or videographer have arrived.

HONORARY DUTIES

TASKS FOR THE HONOR ATTENDANT AND BEST MAN

———— ✳ ————

ALTHOUGH THEIR DUTIES AREN'T SET IN STONE, TRADITIONALLY THE HONOR ATTENDANT AND BEST MAN CAN BE OF SERVICE IN A NUMBER OF AREAS. FEEL FREE TO CUSTOMIZE THESE LISTS FOR YOUR OWN NEEDS.

THE HONOR ATTENDANT

◆ Offers to run errands and assist with the details of planning throughout the engagement period.

◆ Organizes fittings for bridesmaids.

◆ Pays for her own wedding attire.

◆ Helps address invitations.

◆ May host a bachelorette party or bridal shower, alone or with the assistance of the bridesmaids.

◆ Helps the bride dress for the ceremony and change into her going-away clothes at the reception.

◆ Arranges the bride's veil and train before and after her walk down the aisle.

◆ Holds the bride's bouquet during the wedding ceremony.

◆ Holds the groom's ring until the appropriate time in the ceremony.

◆ Signs the marriage certificate.

◆ Helps the bride bustle her gown, remove her veil, or make other adjustments for the reception.

◆ Makes a toast to the bride and groom at the wedding reception.

THE BEST MAN

◆ Offers to run errands or assist with planning details throughout the engagement.

◆ Organizes fittings for the groomsmen.

◆ Helps the groom with accommodations for groomsmen from out-of-town.

◆ Pays for his own attire.

◆ May host the bachelor party, alone or together with the groomsmen.

◆ Gets the groom to the ceremony on time.

◆ Holds bride's ring during the ceremony.

◆ Signs the marriage certificate.

◆ Toasts the bride and groom at the wedding reception.

Looking for a few more details and further guidance? Haven't found all your vendors? Here's where to go for inspiration and information to help you plan your ceremony, reception, and honeymoon.

PUBLICATIONS

Bridal Bargains
By Denise and Alan Fields
(Windsor Peak Press, 1990)
Help with selecting and prioritizing the most important elements of your celebration, with emphasis on cutting costs.

Bride's Guide to Emotional Survival
By Rita Bigel-Casher
(Prima Publishing, 1996)
Provides reassurance that the stress and pressures you may be feeling are typical during this time, and encourages delegation of responsibilities to friends and family.

Bride's Thank You Guide
By Pamela A. Piljac
(Chicago Review Press, 1993)
Full of sample letters and tips on how to write great thank-you notes for every situation.

Complete Book of Wedding Vows
By Diane Warner
(Career Press, 1996)
Help for writing all or a portion of your own vows.

Emily Post's Complete Book of Wedding Etiquette
By Elizabeth L. Post
(HarperCollins, 1991)
Everything you need to know about wedding etiquette.

Bridal Showers: 50 Great Ideas for a Perfect Shower
By Sharon E. Dlugosch
and Florence E. Nelson
(Putnam, 1987)
A guide to fun, inventive bridal showers and all manner of brides-maids' parties.

Festive Flowers
By Paula Pryke
(Rizzoli International Publications, 1997)
A guide to floral bouquets and arrangements that you can show your florist or use for your own source of inspiration.

Groom's Survival Manual
By Michael R. Perry
(Pocket Books, 1991)
Dedicated to the groom, this concise guide to all of his responsibilities makes a perfect engagement present.

I'm in the Wedding, Too
By Caroline Plaisted
(Dutton Children's Books, 1997)
A keepsake describing the duties of flower girls and junior bridesmaids; includes illustrated pages with space to write or draw.

Modern Bride Honeymoons and Weddings Away
By Geri Bain
(John Wiley & Sons, 1995)
Full of location suggestions and help-ful hints on choosing the perfect locations for honeymoons and desti-nation weddings.

The 100 Best Honeymoon Resorts of the World
By Katharine D. Dyson
(Globe Pequot Press, 1996)
Thoughtfully researched and guar-anteed to motivate you in the right direction; includes hotel and resort contact information along with experienced travelers' comments.

Tabletops: Easy, Practical, Beautiful Ways to Decorate the Table
By Barbara Milo Ohrbach
(Clarkson Potter, 1997)
Perfect for the home wedding; how to decorate by incorporating personal collections and a surprising variety of eclectic containers.

Tussie-Mussies: The Victorian Art of Expressing Yourself in the Language of Flowers
By Geraldine Adamich Laufer
(Workman Publishing Co., 1993)
A full array of Victorian-inspired bouquets and nosegays.

The Wedding Dress
By Maria McBride-Mellinger
(Random House, 1993)
Find inspiration and details for bridal gowns in this beautifully photographed book.

Wedding Speeches and Toasts
By Angela Lansbury
(Ward Lock, 1994)
Sample toasts, including tips for the whole wedding party on preparing and delivering memorable toasts and congratulations.

Bon Appétit magazine
(800) 765-9419
Tear out articles of menu and entertaining ideas you like and show them to your caterer and bridal consultant to describe your tastes.

Brides magazine
(800) 456-6162
All manner of nuptial advice, plus the latest news on wedding trends and fashions—and what other brides are doing and saying.

Elegant Bride magazine
(910) 378-6065
Tips and ideas for the bride-to-be.

Modern Bride magazine
(800) 777-5786
Another useful guide to what's new on the wedding scene.

Honeymoon magazine
(800) 513-7112
Chock-full of destination spots, travelers' tips, and romantic ideas; the two of you can browse through its issues over dinner.

Martha Stewart Living:Weddings
(800) 999-6518
These special editions of the magazine are full of wedding favor ideas; menus; dresses; and photographs of floral designs, cakes, and bouquets.

SUPPLIERS
Carey International Limousine Service
(800) 336-4646
www.careyint.com
A limousine service that also provides transportation, including sedans, vans, and minibuses.

Godiva
(800) 946-3482
www.godiva.com
A chocolatier that delivers beautifully wrapped favors and gifts overnight.

Imperial Gown Restoration Co.
(888) 469-6100
(703) 573-4696
www.wedgown.com
Wedding gown restoration and preservation experts who pick up, clean, preserve, and deliver your gown back to you, with a 50-year replacement-value warranty on their services.

International Currency Express
(888) 278-6628 on the West Coast
(888) 842-0880 on the East Coast
www.foreignmoney.com
If you're traveling abroad on your honeymoon, have local currency delivered to your door, usually within two to three days.

Resource One
(818) 343-3451
Call for a sample package of beautiful tablecloths, napkins, and slipcovers available for rent.

The Social Secretary
(212) 956-2707
www.socialsecretary.com
Call for a list of stationery stores in your area that offer computerized calligraphy, or purchase a calligraphy software package so that you can do it yourself.

Mrs. John L. Strong Fine Stationery
699 Madison Avenue
New York, New York 10021
(212) 838-3775
A tradition of expert advice and hand-engraved stationery.

ORGANIZATIONS
American Rental Association
(800) 334-2177
www.ararental.org
Contact this group for party-supply stores in your area.

Association of Bridal Consultants
200 Chestnut Land Road
New Milford, CT 06776-2521
(860) 355-0464
www.weddingchannel.com
This service provides referrals for professional bridal consultants in your geographic area.

International Formalwear Association
(312) 644-6610
www.formalwear.org
Referrals for men's formal-wear establishments in your area.

Society for Calligraphy
(213) 931-6146
This group will refer you to talented calligraphers in your area.

WORLD WIDE WEB
iBride
www.iBride.com
Continuing discussion groups, along with access to other brides' experiences and advice.

The Knot: Weddings for the Real World
www.theknot.com
The ultimate online wedding guide, including a section for grooms, budget templates, and music suggestions.

INDEX

ACKNOWLEDGMENTS

ADDITIONAL PHOTOGRAPHY: **Barbara Alper** 40, 88, 95. **Woodfin Camp** 115 Israel Talby. **FPG** 16 Michael Hannau; 26 Willie Hill; 27 Seth Joel; 65 Ulf Sjostedt. **Index Stock** 74 Benelux Press; 91 Raeanne Rubenstein. **International Stock** 17 Julian Cotton; 60 Michael Paras; 105 Cliff Hollenbeck. **Stock Market** 111 Chuck Savage. **Tony Stone Images** 31 Sylvain Grandam; 58 Renee Lynn; 83 Stewart Cohen; 98 Dale Durfee; 106 Kaluzney/Thatcher. **Superstock** 14 F. Cruz; 87 K. Zikomo. **Jenny Thomas** 43. **Uniphoto** 78 Don Corning. **Westlight** 34 Bill Varie; 71 Chase Swift. Author photo by Peter Lau. SPECIAL THANKS: The publishers wish to thank the following people for their valuable help during the creation of this book: Desne Border, Nancy Carlson, Rick Clogher, Mandy Erickson, Ruth Jacobson, Dawn Margolis, Cynthia Rubin, Carrie Spector, Patrick Tucker, and Laurie Wertz for editorial assistance; Gigi Haycock for help with photo styling; Paul Rauschelbach for computing support; Sharon Smith for jacket design; Carol Stermer for artist representation; Bill and Kristin Wurz for design assistance; Ken DellaPenta for indexing. Thanks also to Ann Fiedler Creations (Beverly Hills, CA) for the loan of photographic props. AUTHOR'S ACKNOWLEDGMENTS: Without this wonderful support system, the words or energy for this book would never have come together. It was truly a team effort. I'd like to thank Linda Furino, Roland Fasel, Didier Millet, John Owen, Roger Shaw, Dianne Jacob, Bonnie Monte, Liz Marken, Emma Forge, Angie Gore, Joy Lewis, Lynn Gallagher, Gary Hill, Cheryl Benun, Lanette and Jim Penna, and my wonderful husband, James Baroni.